ROBERT COLWELL'S
Guide to SNOW TRAILS

ROBERT COLWELL'S

Other Books by Robert Colwell
    INTRODUCTION TO BACKPACKING
    INTRODUCTION TO FOOT TRAILS IN AMERICA
    INTRODUCTION TO WATER TRAILS IN AMERICA

Guide to SNOW TRAILS

Stackpole Books

ROBERT COLWELL'S GUIDE TO SNOW TRAILS

Copyright © 1973 by
Robert Colwell

Published by
STACKPOLE BOOKS
Cameron and Kelker Streets
Harrisburg, Pa. 17105

All rights reserved, including the right to reproduce this book or any portions thereof in any form or by any means, electronic or mechanical, including photocopying, recording, or by any information storage and retrieval system, without permission in writing from the publisher. All inquiries should be addressed to Stackpole Books, Cameron and Kelker Streets, Harrisburg, Pennsylvania 17105.

Printed in the U.S.A.

```
Library of Congress Cataloging in Publication Data

Colwell, Robert.
   Robert Colwell's guide to snow trails.

   Includes bibliographical references.
   1. Cross-country skiing--United States--Directions.
I. Title.  II. Guide to snow trails.
GV854.4.C64  1973        796.9'3        73-11147
ISBN 0-8117-1492-6
ISBN 0-8117-2015-2  (pbk.)
```

CONTENTS

CITY-TRAIL INDEX - Finding Snow Trails Near a City 9

INTRODUCTION 25

Chapter 1 SNOW TRAILS 29

The burden of bitter winters. Ancient skis. Frontier communication and survival. Winter sport now. Alpine and Nordic skiing. Ski touring. Equipment selection. Rent or buy. Reference reading. Snowshoeing. Winter hiking. Organizations. Ski Touring Council. Skier classification. Safety. Trail marking. The need filled by this book. Choosing the trails. How to use this book. Reference maps and guides. Publications of interest. Enjoying and protecting our snow trails.

Chapter 2 TRAILS EAST 47

Connecticut — Connecticut walk book. Ski touring in Peoples State Forest. Powder Ridge Ski Area.

Maine — Ski tours by the seashore in Acadia National Park. Trails around Andover from Akers Ski. The Cross Country Ski Place trails. Sugarloaf/USA.

Maryland — Rugged country at New Germany State Park.

Massachusetts — Granville State Forest trails. Hartwell Hill Ski Area. Jug End Resort. 15 miles of trails in Pittsfield State Forest. Wyckoff Park Ski Touring Center.

New Jersey — Restricted area in Stokes State Forest.

New Hampshire — The Balsams Wilderness Ski Area trails. Dartmouth Outing Club and Appalachian Trail ski touring. Franconia Inn and their ski touring center. Franconia Notch State Park. Gray Ledges, a Christian conference and retreat. Jackson, the first ski touring community in the nation. Loon Mountain. Ski touring trails out of Pinkham Notch Camp. Temple Mountain Ski Area. Waterville Valley, good ski touring trails. Windblown, a ski touring center.

New York — Adirondak Loj, trails into the mountains. Bear Mountain State Park, trails close to New York City. Big Tupper Ski Area. Erie Bridge Cross Country Ski Center and trails. Charming Fo'castle Farms. Frost Ridge. Happy Valley Ski Center at Alfred University. Mr. Moose Outfitters. Pine Ridge Ski Area. Rum Runner Ski Touring Center. Swain Ski Center. West Mountain.

Pennsylvania — Blue Knob Ski Area. Crystal Lake Camp and Conference Center. Elk Mountain Ski Center. Mount Airy Lodge, a complete resort. Seven Springs.

Vermont — Blueberry Hill Farm, a wonderful informal ski touring center. Burke Mountain. Dakins Vermont Mountain Shop had it all for ski tourers. The Farm Motor Inn and Country Club, a unique New England farm. Killington, Madonna Ski Area. Mountain Meadows Lodge has a ski touring center. Moun-

CONTENTS • 7

tain Top Inn. Mount Snow. Okemo. Sawmill Farm and its ski touring center. Stowe Center, headquarters for North American Nordic Ski Touring System. Stratton Mountain. Sugarbush Inn has it all. Trapp Family Lodge, probably the first organized ski touring center in America. Viking Ski Touring Center. Woody's Cracker Barrel, a familiar home to all eastern ski tourers.

Virginia — Shenandoah National Park. The Blue Ridge Parkway. Sea and Ski Shop, Ltd.

Chapter 3   TRAILS MIDWEST   107

Iowa — Postville AYH. Walden Pond.

Michigan — Boyne Mountain. Michigan Riding and Hiking Trails. Porcupine Mountain Wilderness State Park. Trails at Ishpeming, birthplace of the National Ski Association.

Minnesota — Equinox Ski Touring Club, a complete center. Hidden Valley. Sugar Hills.

Wisconsin — Gateway Hotel and Inn. Hardscrabble Ski Area. Ski touring trails in Nicolet National Forest. Nor-Ski Ridge. Great trails in North Kettle Moraine Forest. Port Mountain. Telemark Lodge. Whitecap Mountains.

Chapter 4   TRAILS WEST   123

Arizona — Williams Ski Area

Colorado — Ashcroft Ski Tours Unlimited, a mountain touring center near Aspen. The Alpineer Ski Touring Center. Trails in Pike National Forest. Ptarmigan Tours, a center. Rocky Mountain Expeditions, tours in the Rocky Mountains. Rocky Mountain National Park trails. Rocky Mountain Ski Tours. Saylor Park Ski Touring Area. Scandinavian Lodge, a complete ski touring center. Trails in the Shadow Mountain National Recreation Area. Vail. Wilderness Alliance and their long ski tours. Winter Park and trails near the Continental Divide.

Idaho — Robinson Bar Ranch for ski tourers.

Montana — Big Mountain. Big Sky, where the emphasis is on ski touring. Bridger Bowl. Glacier National Park. Libby and the trails in the Cabinet Mountain Wilderness Area.

New Mexico — Sandia Recreation Area. Trails overlooking Albuquerque. Sipapu Lodge and trails at high elevations. Taos Ski Valley.

Utah — Park City. Snowland in the beautiful high country.

Wyoming — Happy Jack Ski Area. Jackson Hole, a ski tourer's delight. Medicine Bow Ski Area. Restricted area in Shoshone National Forest. Yellowstone National Park, one of the very best ski touring areas in America.

Chapter 5 TRAILS FAR WEST 157

California — Alpine Meadows and its complete program. Boreal Ridge. Cal-Nordic Ski Touring Institute, none better. Kirkwood Ski Touring Center, with everything for the winter experience. Trails at Lassen Volcanic National Park. The majesty of the big trees at Sequoia and Kings Canyon National Parks. Yosemite National Park, a wonderland for the ski tourer.

Oregon — Anthony Lakes. Cooper Spur on the north side of Mt. Hood. Crater Lake National Park, trails around the beautiful lake. A restricted area at Diamond Lake. Hoodo Bowl. Mt. Bachelor Ski Area, a downhill area with a well developed ski touring program. Spout Springs. Trillium Lake Basin near Mt. Hood.

Washington — 49° North. Mission Ridge and good ski touring. Mt. Baker has summer skiing. Mount Rainier National Park trails. Ski Hurricane Ridge at Olympic National Park.

INDEX   181

CITY-TRAIL INDEX

Finding Snow Trails Near a City

In selecting snow trails for this book consideration was given to the proximity of urban areas. Below each city in the following index are listed those snow trail areas within a 125-mile radius, or about 3 hours' driving time, from a city. In some cases the radius has been stretched. This index includes over 100 cities, 70 of which have been selected from the 150 cities in America with populations over 100,000.

AKRON, Ohio
    Blue Knob Ski Area   90
    Happy Valley Ski Center   82
    New Germany State Park   56
    Seven Springs   89
    Swain Ski Center   85

ALBANY, New York
    Adirondak Loj   75
    Balsams Wilderness Ski Area   65

    Bark Eater   79
    Bear Mountain State Park   78
    Big Tupper Ski Area   79
    Blueberry Hill Farm   91
    Burke Mountain   93
    Dakin's Vermont Mountain Shop   95
    Dartmouth Outing Club   66
    Erie Bridge Cross Country Ski
        Center   80
    Farm Motor Inn and Country Club   95

CITY-TRAIL INDEX

ALBANY, New York (Cont. page 10)
Fo'castle Farms 81
Franconia Inn 66
Franconia Notch State Park 67
Frost Ridge 82
Granville State Forest 58
Gray Ledges 68
Happy Valley Ski Center 82
Hartwell Hill Ski Area 58
Inlet and Old Forge 83
Jackson 68
Jug End Resort 59
Killington 96
Loon Mountain 70
Madonna Ski Area 97
Mr. Moose Outfitters 83
Mountain Meadows Lodge 97
Mountain Top Inn 99
Mount Snow 99
Okemo 100
Peoples State Forest 48
Pine Ridge Ski Area 84
Pinkham Notch Camp 70
Pittsfield State Forest 60
Powder Ridge Ski Area 49
Rum Runner Ski Touring Center 84
Saw Mill Farm 101
Stowe Center 101
Stratton Mountain 102
Sugarbush Inn 103
Temple Mountain Ski Area 72
Trapp Family Lodge 104
Viking Ski Touring Center 105
Waterville Valley 73
West Mountain 86
Windblown 74
Woody's Cracker Barrel 106
Wyckoff Park Ski Touring Center 62

ALBUQUERQUE, New Mexico
Sandia Recreation Area 142
Sipapu Lodge 143
Taos Ski Valley 144
Trail Adventures de Chama 145

ALEXANDRIA, Virginia
Blue Knob Ski Area 90
Blue Ridge Parkway 106
Crystal Lake Camp and Conference Center 87
Elk Mountain Ski Center 88
Mount Airy Lodge 88
New Germany State Park 56
Shenandoah National Park 106
Stokes State Forest 63

ALLENTOWN, Pennsylvania
Bear Mountain State Park 78
Blue Knob Ski Area 90
Crystal Lake Camp and Conference Center 87
Elk Mountain Ski Center 88
Mount Airy Lodge 88
New Germany State Park 56
Peoples State Forest 48
Powder Ridge Ski Area 49
Stokes State Forest 63

AUGUSTA, Maine
Acadia National Park 50
Akers Ski 52
Balsams Wilderness Ski Area 65
Cross Country Ski Place 53
Dartmouth Outing Club 66
Franconia Inn 66
Franconia Notch State Park 67
Gray Ledges 68
Jackson 68
Loon Mountain 70
Pinkham Notch Camp 70
Squaw Mountain 54
Sugarloaf/USA 54
Temple Mountain Ski Area 72
Waterville Valley 73
Windblown 74

BALTIMORE, Maryland
Blue Knob Ski Area 90
Blue Ridge Parkway 106
Crystal Lake Camp and Conference Center 87
Elk Mountain Ski Center 88
Mount Airy Lodge 88

Stowe Ski Touring Center, Vermont

CITY-TRAIL INDEX

BALTIMORE, Maryland (Cont.)
New Germany State Park 56
Shenandoah National Park 106
Stokes State Forest 63

BANGOR, Maine
Acadia National Park 50
Akers Ski 52
Balsams Wilderness Ski Area 65
Cross Country Ski Place 53
Franconia Inn 66
Franconia Notch State Park 67
Jackson 68
Loon Mountain 70
Pinkham Notch Camp 70
Squaw Mountain 54
Sugarloaf/USA 54
Waterville Valley 73

BEND, Oregon
Anthony Lakes 158
Cooper Spur 159
Crater Lake National Park 159
Diamond Lake 160
Hoodo Bowl 160
Mt. Bachelor Ski Area 162
Spout Springs 163
Sunriver 164
Trillium Lake Basin 164

BERKELEY, California
Alpine Meadows 172
Boreal Ridge 173
Cal-Nordic Ski Touring Institute 173
Donner Ski Ranch 174
Kirkwood Ski Touring Center 175
Lassen Volcanic National Park 176
Sequoia and Kings Canyon National Parks 177
Yosemite National Park 178

BILLINGS, Montana
Big Mountain 137
Big Sky 138
Bridger Bowl 138
Cooke City 141
Happy Jack Ski Area 149
Jackson Hole 151
Yellowstone National Park 155

BINGHAMTON, New York
Adirondak Loj 75
Bark Eater 79
Bear Mountain State Park 78
Big Tupper Ski Area 79
Blue Knob Ski Area 90
Crystal Lake Camp and Conference Center 87
Elk Mountain Ski Center 88
Erie Bridge Cross Country Ski Center 80
Fo'castle Farms 81
Frost Ridge 82
Happy Valley Ski Center 82
Inlet and Old Forge 83
Jug End Resort 59
Mr. Moose Outfitters 83
Mount Airy Lodge 88
Peoples State Forest 48
Pine Ridge Ski Area 84
Pittsfield State Forest 60
Rum Runner Ski Touring Center 84
Stokes State Forest 63
Swain Ski Center 85
West Mountain 86

BISHOP, California
Alpine Meadows 172
Boreal Ridge 173
Cal-Nordic Ski Touring Institute 173
Donner Ski Ranch 174
Kirkwood Ski Touring Center 175
Sequoia and Kings Canyon National Parks 177
Yosemite National Park 178

BOSTON, Massachusetts
Balsams Wilderness Ski Area 65
Blueberry Hill Farm 91
Burke Mountain 93
Dakin's Vermont Mountain Shop 95
Dartmouth Outing Club 66
Farm Motor Inn and Country Club 95

CITY-TRAIL INDEX • 13

Franconia Inn 66
Franconia Notch State Park 67
Granville State Forest 58
Gray Ledges 68
Hartwell Hill Ski Area 58
Jackson 68
Jug End Resort 59
Killington 96
Loon Mountain 70
Madonna Ski Area 97
Mountain Meadows Lodge 97
Mountain Top Inn 99
Mount Snow 99
Okemo 100
Peoples State Forest 48
Pinkham Notch Camp 70
Pittsfield State Forest 60
Powder Ridge Ski Area 49
Saw Mill Farm 101
Stowe Center 101
Stratton Mountain 102
Sugarbush Inn 103
Temple Mountain Ski Area 72
Trapp Family Lodge 104
Viking Ski Touring Center 105
Waterville Valley 73
Waubeeka Spring 61
Windblown 74
Woody's Cracker Barrel 106
Wyckoff Park Ski Touring Center 62

BRIDGEPORT, Connecticut
Bear Mountain State Park 78
Blue Knob Ski Area 90
Crystal Lake Camp and Conference
   Center 87
Elk Mountain Ski Center 88
Fo'castle Farms 81
Granville State Forest 58
Hartwell Hill Ski Area 58
Jug End Resort 59
Mount Airy Lodge 88
Peoples State Forest 48
Pittsfield State Forest 60
Powder Ridge Ski Area 49
Seven Springs 89

Stokes State Forest 63
Waubeeka Spring 61
Wyckoff Park Ski Touring Center 62

BUFFALO, New York
Erie Bridge Cross Country Ski
   Center 80
Frost Ridge 82
Happy Valley Ski Center 82
Seven Springs 89
Swain Ski Center 85

BUTTE, Montana
Big Mountain 137
Big Sky 138
Bridger Bowl 138
Cooke City 141
Glacier National Park 140
Libby 141
Yellowstone National Park 155

CAMDEN, New Jersey
Bear Mountain State Park 78
Blue Knob Ski Area 90
Crystal Lake Camp and Conference
   Center 87
Elk Mountain Ski Center 88
Mount Airy Lodge 88
New Germany State Park 56
Stokes State Forest 63

CANTON, Ohio
Blue Knob Ski Area 90
Happy Valley Ski Center 82
New Germany State Park 56
Seven Springs 89
Swain Ski Center 85

CEDAR RAPIDS, Iowa
Postville AYH 109
Walden Pond 109

CHARLESTON, West Virginia
Blue Ridge Parkway 106
Shenandoah National Park 106

14 • CITY-TRAIL INDEX

CHEYENNE, Wyoming
Happy Jack Ski Area 149
Medicine Bow Ski Area 153
Rocky Mountain Expeditions 129
Rocky Mountain National Park 129
Rocky Mountain Ski Tours 131
Scandinavian Lodge 131
Shadow Mountain National Recreation
  Area 132
Wilderness Alliance 133
Winter Park 135

CHICAGO, Illinois
North Kettle Moraine Forest 119
Postville AYH 109
Walden Pond 109

CLEVELAND, Ohio
Blue Knob Ski Area 90
Happy Valley Ski Center 82
New Germany State Park 56
Seven Springs 89
Swain Ski Center 85

COLORADO SPRINGS, Colorado
Alpineer, The 126
Ashcroft Ski Tours Unlimited 125
Pike National Forest 127
Ptarmigan Tours 127
Rocky Mountain Expeditions 129
Rocky Mountain National Park 129
Rocky Mountain Ski Tours 131
Saylor Park Ski Touring Area 127
Scandinavian Lodge 131
Shadow Mountain National Recreation
  Area 132
Vail 133
Wilderness Alliance 133
Winter Park 135

DENVER, Colorado
Alpineer, The 126
Ashcroft Ski Tours Unlimited 125
Happy Jack Ski Area 149
Medicine Bow Ski Area 153

Pike National Forest 127
Ptarmigan Tours 127
Rocky Mountain Expeditions 129
Rocky Mountain National Park 129
Rocky Mountain Ski Tours 131
Saylor Park Ski Touring Area 127
Scandinavian Lodge 131
Shadow Mountain National Recreation
  Area 132
Vail 133
Wilderness Alliance 133
Winter Park 135

DES MOINES, Iowa
Postville AYH 109
Walden Pond 109

DETROIT, Michigan
Boyne Mountain 109
Michigan Riding and Hiking Trail 111

DUBUQUE, Iowa
North Kettle Moraine Forest 119
Postville AYH 109
Walden Pond 109

DULUTH, Minnesota
Equinox Ski Touring Club 113
Gateway Hotel and Inn 116
Hardscrabble Ski Area 115
Hidden Valley 114
Nicolet National Forest 117
Port Mountain 120
Sugar Hills 114
Telemark Lodge 121
Whitecap Mountains 120

ELIZABETH, New Jersey
Bear Mountain State Park 78
Blue Knob Ski Area 90
Crystal Lake Camp and Conference
  Center 87
Elk Mountain Ski Center 88
Fo'castle Farms 81
Jug End Resort 59
Mount Airy Lodge 88

Peoples State Forest 48
Pittsfield State Forest 60
Powder Ridge Ski Area 49
Stokes State Forest 63

ERIE, Pennsylvania
Blue Knob Ski Area 90
Erie Bridge Cross Country Ski Center 80
Happy Valley Ski Center 82
New Germany State Park 56
Seven Springs 89
Swain Ski Center 85

EUGENE, Oregon
Anthony Lakes 158
Cooper Spur 159
Crater Lake National Park 159
Diamond Lake 160
Hoodo Bowl 160
Mt. Bachelor Ski Area 162
Spout Springs 163
Sunriver 164
Trillium Lake Basin 164

EUREKA, California
Crater Lake National Park 159
Lassen Volcanic National Park 176

FARMINGTON, New Mexico
Sandia Recreation Area 142
Sipapu Lodge 143
Taos Ski Valley 144
Trail Adventures de Chama 145

FLINT, Michigan
Boyne Mountain 109
Michigan Riding and Hiking Trail 111

FRESNO, California
Alpine Meadows 172
Boreal Ridge 173
Cal-Nordic Ski Touring Institute 173
Donner Ski Ranch 174
Kirkwood Ski Touring Center 175

Sequoia and Kings Canyon National Parks 177
Yosemite National Park 178

GRAND JUNCTION, Colorado
Alpineer, The 126
Ashcroft Ski Tours Unlimited 125
Ptarmigan Tours 127
Vail 133

GRAND RAPIDS, Michigan
Boyne Mountain 109
Michigan Riding and Hiking Trail 111

GREAT FALLS, Montana
Big Mountain 137
Big Sky 138
Bridger Bowl 138
Glacier National Park 140
Libby 141

GREEN BAY, Wisconsin
Gateway Hotel and Inn 116
Hardscrabble Ski Area 115
Ishpeming 110
Nicolet National Forest 117
Nor-Ski Ridge 117
North Kettle Moraine Forest 119

HARRISBURG, Pennsylvania
Bear Mountain State Park 78
Blue Knob Ski Area 90
Crystal Lake Camp and Conference Center 87
Elk Mountain Ski Center 88
Mount Airy Lodge 88
New Germany State Park 56
Seven Springs 89
Shenandoah National Park 106
Stokes State Forest 63

HARTFORD, Connecticut
Balsams Wilderness Ski Area 65
Bear Mountain State Park 78
Blueberry Hill Farm 91
Burke Mountain 93

CITY-TRAIL INDEX

HARTFORD, Connecticut (Cont.)

Dakin's Vermont Mountain Shop 95
Dartmouth Outing Club 66
Farm Motor Inn and Country Club 95
Fo'castle Farms 81
Franconia Inn 66
Franconia Notch State Park 67
Granville State Forest 58
Gray Ledges 68
Hartwell Hill Ski Area 58
Jackson 68
Jug End Resort 59
Killington 96
Loon Mountain 70
Madonna Ski Area 97
Mr. Moose Outfitters 83
Mountain Meadows Lodge 97
Mountain Top Inn 99
Mount Snow 99
Okemo 100
Peoples State Forest 48
Pinkham Notch Camp 70
Pittsfield State Forest 60
Powder Ridge Ski Area 49
Saw Mill Farm 101
Stowe Center 101
Stratton Mountain 102
Sugarbush Inn 103
Temple Mountain Ski Area 72
Trapp Family Lodge 104
Viking Ski Touring Center 105
Waterville Valley 73
Waubeeka Spring 61
Windblown 74
Woody's Cracker Barrel 106
Wyckoff Park Ski Touring Center 62

IDAHO FALLS, Idaho

Big Sky 138
Jackson Hole 151
Robinson Bar Ranch 136
Shoshone National Forest 155
Yellowstone National Park 155

IRONWOOD, Michigan

Gateway Hotel and Inn 116

Hardscrabble Ski Area 115
Ishpeming 110
Nicolet National Forest 117
Porcupine Mountain Wilderness State Park 112
Port Mountain 120
Telemark Lodge 121
Whitecap Mountains 120

JACKSON, Wyoming

Big Mountain 137
Big Sky 138
Bridger Bowl 138
Cooke City 141
Shoshone National Forest 155
Yellowstone National Park 155

JERSEY CITY, New Jersey

Bear Mountain State Park 78
Blue Knob Ski Area 90
Crystal Lake Camp and Conference Center 87
Elk Mountain Ski Center 88
Fo'castle Farms 81
Jug End Resort 59
Mount Airy Lodge 88
Peoples State Forest 48
Pittsfield State Forest 60
Powder Ridge Ski Area 49
Stokes State Forest 63
Waubeeka Spring 61

LA CROSSE, Wisconsin

Equinox Ski Touring Club 113
Gateway Hotel and Inn 116
Hardscrabble Ski Area 115
Nicolet National Forest 117
Nor-Ski Ridge 117
North Kettle Moraine Forest 119
Port Mountain 120
Postville AYH 109
Telemark Lodge 121
Walden Pond 109
Whitecap Mountains 120

CITY-TRAIL INDEX • 17

LANSING, Michigan
Boyne Mountain 109
Michigan Riding and Hiking Trail 111

LAS VEGAS, Nevada
Williams Ski Area 125

LIVONIA, Michigan
Boyne Mountain 109
Michigan Riding and Hiking Trail 111

MADISON, Wisconsin
Nor-Ski Ridge 117
North Kettle Moraine Forest 119
Postville AYH 109
Walden Pond 109

MARQUETTE, Michigan
Gateway Hotel and Inn 116
Ishpeming 110
Nicolet National Forest 117
Nor-Ski Ridge 117
Porcupine Mountain Wilderness State Park 112
Port Mountain 120
Whitecap Mountains 120

MERCED, California
Alpine Meadows 172
Boreal Ridge 173
Cal-Nordic Ski Touring Institute 173
Donner Ski Ranch 174
Kirkwood Ski Touring Center 175
Sequoia and Kings Canyon National Parks 177
Yosemite National Park 178

MILWAUKEE, Wisconsin
Nor-Ski Ridge 117
North Kettle Moraine Forest 119
Postville AYH 109
Walden Pond 109

MINNEAPOLIS, Minnesota
Equinox Ski Touring Club 113
Hardscrabble Ski Area 115
Hidden Valley 114
North Kettle Moraine Forest 119
Port Mountain 120
Sugar Hills 114
Telemark Lodge 121
Whitecap Mountains 120

NEWARK, New Jersey
Bear Mountain State Park 78
Blue Knob Ski Area 90
Crystal Lake Camp and Conference Center 87
Elk Mountain Ski Center 88
Fo'castle Farms 81
Jug End Resort 59
Mount Airy Lodge 88
Peoples State Forest 48
Pittsfield State Forest 60
Powder Ridge Ski Area 49
Stokes State Forest 63
Waubeeka Spring 61

NEW BEDFORD, Massachusetts
Balsams Wilderness Ski Area 65
Blueberry Hill Farm 91
Burke Mountain 93
Dakin's Vermont Mountain Shop 95
Dartmouth Outing Club 66
Farm Motor Inn and Country Club 95
Franconia Inn 66
Franconia Notch State Park 67
Granville State Forest 58
Gray Ledges 68
Hartwell Hill Ski Area 58
Jackson 68
Jug End Resort 59
Killington 96
Loon Mountain 70
Madonna Ski Area 97
Mountain Meadows Lodge 97
Mountain Top Inn 99
Mount Snow 99

CITY-TRAIL INDEX

NEW BEDFORD, Massachusetts (Cont.)
Okemo 100
Peoples State Forest 48
Pinkham Notch Camp 70
Pittsfield State Forest 60
Powder Ridge Ski Area 49
Saw Mill Farm 101
Stowe Center 101
Stratton Mountain 102
Sugarbush Inn 103
Temple Mountain Ski Area 72
Trapp Family Lodge 104
Viking Ski Touring Center 105
Waterville Valley 73
Waubeeka Spring 61
Windblown 74
Woody's Cracker Barrel 106
Wyckoff Park Ski Touring Center 62

NEW HAVEN, Connecticut
Balsams Wilderness Ski Area 65
Bear Mountain State Park 78
Blueberry Hill Farm 91
Burke Mountain 93
Dakin's Vermont Mountain Shop 95
Dartmouth Outing Club 66
Farm Motor Inn and Country Club 95
Fo'castle Farms 81
Franconia Inn 66
Franconia Notch State Park 67
Granville State Forest 58
Gray Ledges 68
Hartwell Hill Ski Area 58
Jackson 68
Jug End Resort 59
Killington 96
Loon Mountain 70
Madonna Ski Area 97
Mr. Moose Outfitters 83
Mountain Meadows Lodge 97
Mountain Top Inn 99
Mount Snow 99
Okemo 100
Peoples State Forest 48
Pinkham Notch Camp 70

Pittsfield State Forest 60
Powder Ridge Ski Area 49
Saw Mill Farm 101
Stowe Center 101
Stratton Mountain 102
Sugarbush Inn 103
Temple Mountain Ski Area 72
Trapp Family Lodge 104
Viking Ski Touring Center 105
Waterville Valley 73
Waubeeka Spring 61
Windblown 74
Woody's Cracker Barrel 106
Wyckoff Park Ski Touring Center 62

NEWPORT NEWS, Virginia
Blue Ridge Parkway 106
Shenandoah National Park 106

NEW YORK, New York
Bear Mountain State Park 78
Blue Knob Ski Area 90
Crystal Lake Camp and Conference Center 87
Elk Mountain Ski Center 88
Fo'castle Farms 81
Jug End Resort 59
Mount Airy Lodge 88
Peoples State Forest 48
Pittsfield State Forest 60
Powder Ridge Ski Area 49
Stokes State Forest 63
Waubeeka Spring 61

NORFOLK, Virginia
Blue Ridge Parkway 106
Shenandoah National Park 106

OAKLAND, California
Alpine Meadows 172
Boreal Ridge 173
Cal-Nordic Ski Touring Institute 173
Donner Ski Ranch 174
Kirkwood Ski Touring Center 175
Lassen Volcanic National Park 176

CITY-TRAIL INDEX • 19

Sequoia and Kings Canyon National Parks 177
Yosemite National Park 178

OLYMPIA, Washington
Cooper Spur 159
49° North 165
Mission Ridge 165
Mt. Baker 167
Mount Rainier National Park 169
Olympic National Park 170

PATERSON, New Jersey
Bear Mountain State Park 78
Blue Knob Ski Area 90
Crystal Lake Camp and Conference Center 87
Elk Mountain Ski Center 88
Fo'castle Farms 81
Jug End Resort 59
Mount Airy Lodge 88
Peoples State Forest 48
Pittsfield State Forest 60
Powder Ridge Ski Area 49
Stokes State Forest 63
Waubeeka Spring 61

PHILADELPHIA, Pennsylvania
Bear Mountain State Park 78
Blue Knob Ski Area 90
Crystal Lake Camp and Conference Center 87
Elk Mountain Ski Center 88
Mount Airy Lodge 88
New Germany State Park 56
Seven Springs 89
Shenandoah National Park 106
Stokes State Forest 63

PHOENIX, Arizona
Williams Ski Area 125

PITTSBURGH, Pennsylvania
Blue Knob Ski Area 90
Blue Ridge Parkway 106

New Germany State Park 56
Seven Springs 89
Shenandoah National Park 106

POCATELLO, Idaho
Big Sky 138
Jackson Hole 151
Robinson Bar Ranch 136
Shoshone National Forest 155
Yellowstone National Park 155

PORTLAND, Maine
Acadia National Park 50
Akers Ski 52
Balsams Wilderness Ski Area 65
Blueberry Hill Farm 91
Burke Mountain 93
Cross Country Ski Place 53
Dakin's Vermont Mountain Shop 95
Dartmouth Outing Club 66
Farm Motor Inn and Country Club 95
Franconia Inn 66
Franconia Notch State Park 67
Gray Ledges 68
Hartwell Hill Ski Area 58
Jackson 68
Killington 96
Loon Mountain 70
Madonna Ski Area 97
Mountain Meadows Lodge 97
Mountain Top Inn 99
Mount Snow 99
Okemo 100
Peoples State Forest 48
Pinkham Notch Camp 70
Powder Ridge Ski Area 49
Saw Mill Farm 101
Squaw Mountain 54
Stowe Center 101
Stratton Mountain 102
Sugarbush Inn 103
Sugarloaf/USA 54
Temple Mountain Ski Area 72
Trapp Family Lodge 104
Viking Ski Touring Center 105

CITY-TRAIL INDEX

PORTLAND, Maine (Cont.)
  Waterville Valley   73
  Windblown   74
  Woody's Cracker Barrel   106
  Wyckoff Park Ski Touring Center   62

PORTLAND, Oregon
  Anthony Lakes   158
  Cooper Spur   159
  Crater Lake National Park   159
  Diamond Lake   160
  Hoodo Bowl   160
  Mission Ridge   165
  Mt. Bachelor Ski Area   162
  Mt. Rainier National Park   169
  Spout Springs   163
  Trillium Lake Basin   164

PORTSMOUTH, Virginia
  Blue Ridge Parkway   106
  Shenandoah National Park   106

PROVIDENCE, Rhode Island
  Balsams Wilderness Ski Area   65
  Blueberry Hill Farm   91
  Burke Mountain   93
  Dakin's Vermont Mountain Shop   95
  Dartmouth Outing Club   66
  Farm Motor Inn and Country Club   95
  Franconia Inn   66
  Franconia Notch State Park   67
  Granville State Forest   58
  Gray Ledges   68
  Hartwell Hill Ski Area   58
  Jackson   68
  Jug End Resort   59
  Killington   96
  Loon Mountain   70
  Madonna Ski Area   97
  Mountain Meadows Lodge   97
  Mountain Top Inn   99
  Mount Snow   99
  Okemo   100
  Peoples State Forest   48
  Pinkham Notch Camp   70
  Pittsfield State Forest   60
  Powder Ridge Ski Area   49
  Saw Mill Farm   101
  Stowe Center   101
  Stratton Mountain   102
  Sugarbush Inn   103
  Temple Mountain Ski Area   72
  Trapp Family Lodge   104
  Viking Ski Touring Center   105
  Waterville Valley   73
  Waubeeka Spring   61
  Windblown   74
  Woody's Cracker Barrel   106
  Wyckoff Park Ski Touring Center   62

REDDING, California
  Anthony Lakes   158
  Boreal Ridge   173
  Crater Lake National Park   159
  Donner Ski Ranch   174
  Kirkwood Ski Touring Center   175
  Lassen Volcanic National Park   176

RENO, Nevada
  Anthony Lakes   158
  Boreal Ridge   173
  Donner Ski Ranch   174
  Kirkwood Ski Touring Center   175
  Lassen Volcanic National Park   176
  Yosemite National Park   178

RICHMOND, Virginia
  Blue Ridge Parkway   106
  New Germany State Park   56
  Shenandoah National Park   106

RIFLE, Colorado
  Alpineer, The   126
  Ashcroft Ski Tours Unlimited   125
  Pike National Forest   127
  Ptarmigan Tours   127
  Rocky Mountain Expeditions   129
  Rocky Mountain National Park   129
  Rocky Mountain Ski Tours   131
  Saylor Park Ski Touring Area   127

CITY-TRAIL INDEX • 21

Scandinavian Lodge 131
Shadow Mountain National Recreation
   Area 132
Vail 133
Wilderness Alliance 133
Winter Park 135

ROCHESTER, New York
Erie Bridge Cross Country Ski
   Center 80
Frost Ridge 82
Happy Valley Ski Center 82
Seven Springs 89
Swain Ski Center 85

ROCKFORD, Illinois
North Kettle Moraine Forest 119
Postville AYH 109
Walden Pond 109

ROSWELL, New Mexico
Sandia Recreation Area 142
Sipapu Lodge 143
Taos Ski Valley 144
Trail Adventures de Chama 145

SACRAMENTO, California
Alpine Meadows 172
Boreal Ridge 173
Cal-Nordic Ski Touring Institute 173
Donner Ski Ranch 174
Kirkwood Ski Touring Center 175
Lassen Volcanic National Park 176
Sequoia and Kings Canyon National
   Parks 177
Yosemite National Park 178

ST. PAUL, Minnesota
Equinox Ski Touring Club 113
Hardscrabble Ski Area 115
Hidden Valley 114
North Kettle Moraine Forest 119
Port Mountain 120
Sugar Hills 114
Telemark Lodge 121
Whitecap Mountains 120

SALIDA, Colorado
Alpineer, The 126
Ashcroft Ski Tours Unlimited 125
Pike National Forest 127
Ptarmigan Tours 127
Rocky Mountain Expeditions 129
Rocky Mountain National Park 129
Rocky Mountain Ski Tours 131
Saylor Park Ski Touring Area 127
Scandinavian Lodge 131
Shadow Mountain National Recreation
   Area 132
Vail 133
Wilderness Alliance 133
Winter Park 135

SALT LAKE CITY, Utah
Park City 145
Snowland 147

SAN FRANCISCO and SAN JOSE, California
Alpine Meadows 172
Boreal Ridge 173
Cal-Nordic Ski Touring Institute 173
Donner Ski Ranch 174
Kirkwood Ski Touring Center 175
Lassen Volcanic National Park 176
Sequoia and Kings Canyon National
   Parks 177
Yosemite National Park 178

SANTA FE, New Mexico
Sandia Recreation Area 142
Sipapu Lodge 143
Taos Ski Valley 144
Trail Adventures de Chama 145

SCRANTON, Pennsylvania
Blue Knob Ski Area 90
Crystal Lake Camp and Conference
   Center 87
Elk Mountain Ski Center 88
Erie Bridge Cross Country Ski
   Center 80
Fo'castle Farms 81
Frost Ridge 82

22 • CITY-TRAIL INDEX

SCRANTON, Pennsylvania (Cont.)

Happy Valley Ski Center 82
Mr. Moose Outfitters 83
Mount Airy Lodge 88
Peoples State Forest 48
Pine Ridge Ski Area 84
Rum Runner Ski Touring Center 84
Seven Springs 89
Swain Ski Center 85

SEATTLE, Washington

49° North 165
Mission Ridge 165
Mt. Baker 167
Mount Rainier National Park 169
Olympic National Park 170
Wenatchee National Forest 171

SPRINGFIELD, Massachusetts

Balsams Wilderness Ski Area 65
Bear Mountain State Park 78
Blueberry Hill Farm 91
Burke Mountain 93
Dakin's Vermont Mountain Shop 95
Dartmouth Outing Club 66
Farm Motor Inn and Country Club 95
Fo'castle Farms 81
Franconia Inn 66
Franconia Notch State Park 67
Granville State Forest 58
Gray Ledges 68
Hartwell Hill Ski Area 58
Jackson 68
Jug End Resort 59
Killington 96
Loon Mountain 70
Madonna Ski Area 97
Mr. Moose Outfitters 83
Mountain Meadows Lodge 97
Mountain Top Inn 99
Mount Snow 99
Okemo 100
Peoples State Forest 48
Pinkham Notch Camp 70

Pittsfield State Forest 60
Powder Ridge Ski Area 49
Saw Mill Farm 101
Stowe Center 101
Stratton Mountain 102
Sugarbush Inn 103
Temple Mountain Ski Area 72
Trapp Family Lodge 104
Viking Ski Touring Center 105
Waterville Valley 73
Waubeeka Spring 61
Windblown 74
Woody's Cracker Barrel 106
Wyckoff Park Ski Touring Center 62

STAMFORD, Connecticut

Bear Mountain State Park 78
Blue Knob Ski Area 90
Crystal Lake Camp and Conference Center 87
Elk Mountain Ski Center 88
Fo'castle Farms 81
Jug End Resort 59
Mount Airy Lodge 88
Peoples State Forest 48
Pittsfield State Forest 60
Powder Ridge Ski Area 49
Stokes State Forest 63
Waubeeka Spring 61

STOCKTON, California

Alpine Meadows 172
Boreal Ridge 173
Cal-Nordic Ski Touring Institute 173
Donner Ski Ranch 174
Kirkwood Ski Touring Center 175
Lassen Volcanic National Park 176
Sequoia and Kings Canyon National Parks 177
Yosemite National Park 178

SYRACUSE, New York

Adirondak Loj 75
Bark Eater 79
Bear Mountain State Park 78
Big Tupper Ski Area 79

CITY-TRAIL INDEX • 23

Erie Bridge Cross Country Ski
  Center 80
Fo'castle Farms 81
Frost Ridge 82
Happy Valley Ski Center 82
Inlet and Old Forge 83
Mr. Moose Outfitters 83
Pine Ridge Ski Area 84
Rum Runner Ski Touring Center 84
Swain Ski Center 85
West Mountain 86

TACOMA, Washington
49° North 165
Mission Ridge 165
Mt. Baker 167
Mount Rainier National Park 169
Olympic National Park 170
Wenatchee National Forest 171

TRAVERSE CITY, Michigan
Boyne Mountain 109
Michigan Riding and Hiking Trail 111

TRENTON, New Jersey
Bear Mountain State Park 78
Blue Knob Ski Area 90
Crystal Lake Camp and Conference
  Center 87
Elk Mountain Ski Center 88
Mount Airy Lodge 88
New Germany State Forest 56
Seven Springs 89
Shenandoah National Park 106
Stokes State Forest 63

VIRGINIA BEACH, Virginia
Blue Ridge Parkway 106
Shenandoah National Park 106

WASHINGTON, D.C.
Blue Knob Ski Area 90
Blue Ridge Parkway 106
Crystal Lake Camp and Conference
  Center 87

Elk Mountain Ski Center 88
Mount Airy Lodge 88
New Germany State Park 56
Shenandoah National Park 106
Stokes State Forest 63

WATERBURY, Connecticut
Balsams Wilderness Ski Area 65
Bear Mountain State Park 78
Blueberry Hill Farm 91
Burke Mountain 93
Dakin's Vermont Mountain Shop 95
Dartmouth Outing Club 66
Farm Motor Inn and Country Club 95
Fo'castle Farms 81
Franconia Inn 66
Franconia Notch State Park 67
Granville State Forest 58
Gray Ledges 68
Hartwell Hill Ski Area 58
Jackson 68
Jug End Resort 59
Killington 96
Loon Mountain 70
Madonna Ski Area 97
Mr. Moose Outfitters 83
Mountain Meadows Lodge 97
Mountain Top Inn 99
Mount Snow 99
Okemo 100
Peoples State Forest 48
Pinkham Notch Camp 70
Pittsfield State Forest 60
Powder Ridge Ski Area 49
Saw Mill Farm 101
Stowe Center 101
Stratton Mountain 102
Sugarbush Inn 103
Temple Mountain Ski Area 72
Trapp Family Lodge 104
Viking Ski Touring Center 105
Waterville Valley 73
Waubeeka Spring 61
Windblown 74
Woody's Cracker Barrel 106
Wyckoff Park Ski Touring Center 62

WORCESTER, Massachusetts
Balsams Wilderness Ski Area 65
Blueberry Hill Farm 91
Burke Mountain 93
Dakin's Vermont Mountain Shop 95
Dartmouth Outing Club 66
Farm Motor Inn and Country Club 95
Franconia Inn 66
Franconia Notch State Park 67
Granville State Forest 58
Gray Ledges 68
Hartwell Hill Ski Area 58
Jackson 68
Jug End Resort 59
Killington 96
Loon Mountain 70
Madonna Ski Area 97
Mountain Meadows Lodge 97
Mountain Top Inn 99
Mount Snow 99
Okemo 100
Peoples State Forest 48
Pinkham Notch Camp 70
Pittsfield State Forest 60
Powder Ridge Ski Area 49
Saw Mill Farm 101
Stowe Center 101
Stratton Mountain 102
Sugarbush Inn 103
Temple Mountain Ski Area 72
Trapp Family Lodge 104
Viking Ski Touring Center 105
Waterville Valley 73
Waubeeka Spring 61
Windblown 74
Woody's Cracker Barrel 106
Wyckoff Park Ski Touring Center 62

YAKIMA, Washington
Cooper Spur 159
49° North 165
Mission Ridge 165
Mt. Baker 167
Mount Rainier National Park 169
Olympic National Park 170
Spout Springs 163
Trillium Lake Basin 164
Wenatchee National Forest 171

YONKERS, New York
Bear Mountain State Park 78
Blue Knob Ski Area 90
Crystal Lake Camp and Conference Center 87
Elk Mountain Ski Center 88
Fo'castle Farms 81
Jug End Resort 59
Mount Airy Lodge 88
Peoples State Forest 48
Pittsfield State Forest 60
Powder Ridge Ski Area 49
Stokes State Forest 63
Waubeeka Spring 61

INTRODUCTION

A QUIET SETTLES on the land once the snow comes. Streams are frozen, no leaves rustle in the wind, most of the birds have migrated, and people keep indoors. To some extent industry is muffled and the automobile is garaged. The quiet is good. It can be appreciated along with the fresh savor of frosty air and new vistas.

Winter gives us another perspective; more of the land is apparent. From a ridge an entire valley floor can be seen. Naked hardwood forests reveal hills and summits seldom seen in summer. And above timberline the snow masks the harshness of rock. It is possible to think of this as a time of healing, the land swathed while patiently submitting to its confinement.

And with the first snowfall seven million skiers gather together their gear and head for the slopes. In lesser numbers their cousins slip into toe bindings and take to the countryside. Unplowed

(Courtesy, Wyoming Travel Commission)
Yellowstone National Park

roads, old logging routes and foot trails are all avenues to a singular experience: ski touring.

Ski touring can be a solitary encounter, the skier's presence complementing the landscape. His rhythm of effort is inherent in the forces of nature apparent to him on these occasions. Oftentimes in the winter starkness of the countryside he will see himself as never before. Perhaps this is why we take up the challenge of journeying to remote places. We feel a need to re-identify with roots often abandoned because of our desire to be part of a social order that demands we be a loyal member of the system or suffer its censure.

Too few people seek the experience of being apart. Certainly those who do will want to be on their own or with good friends at these times. This is possible for those with the skills and temperment. The former is available to just about anyone, for ski touring and showshoeing are open to all ages. A lesson or two will master the fundamentals.

However, at first not everyone wants to go it alone or put up with the hardships associated with wilderness outings. Because ski tours are predominantly day outings, and those on weekends, the ideal compromise here is found at ski touring centers and resorts that welcome ski tourers.

This then is a book for the beginner who wants to learn ski touring at places that offer signed and groomed trails, warming huts, guided tours, instruction and rentals, comfortable lodgings and good food at the end of the day. This is also a book for the practiced tourer looking for new trails in his own backyard, or in a state he would like to visit. There are many places listed here and references made to others where the skier can be on his own in uncrowded forests and mountain slopes, free of the restriction of group touring and limiting trail routes.

Above all this is a book for those who want to be a part of the winter scene in a responsible and satisfying way. It is for those who seek strength and renewal from the land. It is for those who believe that a sunny day, a blue sky, a dazzling white countryside and their presence make a singular combination all too seldom experienced.

Touring at Sugarloaf/USA (Photo by Chip Carey)

CHAPTER 1

SNOW TRAVELS

MEN HAVE ALWAYS had to cope with winter snows in northern climes. For ages winter limited travel, in some cases confining men for the duration. Life was bitter under these circumstances. Communication with others was difficult, and men looked for ways to help keep closer ties. No one knows exactly when the first skis were developed. The evidence is that they existed 4,000 years ago in Sweden, and 3,000 years ago in Norway—and earlier in Siberia. In North America the Indians and Eskimos developed their snowshoes and sleds for transportation and communication. Newcomers to America adopted their methods quickly, augmenting the use of skis and horse-drawn sleighs brought from Europe. However, at best, winter travel has always been arduous and uncomfortable.

Today, in much of the world, winter no longer poses the same hardships for people. Winter has become a pleasant season. Equipment and clothing have advanced to the point where outings are safe and comfortable. Recreational snow play has taken many forms. Some of them, like iceboating and snowmobiling, require machines. Winter hiking. snowshoeing and skiing are all for the self-propelled snow enthusiast. By far the most popular of these is skiing.

ALPINE AND NORDIC SKIING

Two broad categories are used to classify recreational and competitive skiing; each requiring different techniques and equipment. Alpine skiing is generally associated with downhill slopes and racing while Nordic skiing includes competitions in cross-country and jumping. Allied with Nordic skiing is Ski Touring, casual cross-country skiing. No competitions here, although many skiers enjoy all three disciplines. This book is for recreational noncompetitive ski tourers, snowshoers and winter hikers. It is also for those Alpine and Nordic skiers who want a change of pace from their more demanding slopes and races.

SKI TOURING

Ski touring is cross-country skiing using narrow, lightweight skis with special boots and bindings that allow the boot heel to rise while the ski remains on the snow. The developed gait is something like slide-walking and very easy to learn. In fact, anyone who is in good health can ski tour. People who have never skied can quickly pick up the technique. It is an excellent family sport.

Ski touring is for those hikers who want a winter activity but shy away from downhill runs. Bicyclists, joggers and walkers will find ski touring the best winter substitute for their continuing physical fitness programs. And ski touring is for Alpine skiers who want a more leisurely pace. Most of all it is for all of those who are looking for a way to better enjoy those winter days outdoors.

None of the dangers inherent in downhill skiing are to be had in touring. No lift lines, crowds and waiting. No expensive gear, lift tickets and lessons. A small backpack filled with a sandwich and a hot thermos of soup, and you are ready for a wonderful outing.

With book in hand and an open field the new skier can easily practice the necessary skills. Or take advantage of the help to be found in the membership of a ski club; good workshops and tips here. For those who want to do their touring from a downhill ski area there are inexpensive lessons available at many of these establishments. And very popular now with ski tourers are the growing number of private lodges and resorts developed just for ski touring, complete with trails, instruction and rentals.

Note—within this classification of ski touring there is further definition: Nordic ski touring and Alpine ski touring, the latter applied to those tours into Alpine country with the use of specialized gear.

Equipment Selection Many styles and models of ski gear are offered by manufacturers, domestic and foreign. There are skis to be waxed, skis with applied mohair skins, and skis featuring a bottom design requiring no waxing. Today ski tourers can choose from inexpensive laminated wooden skis and others made from metals, fiberglass and other synthetics. The same variety of models applies to bindings, boots and poles. Choosing can present something of a dilemma. These subjects are thoroughly discussed in how-to books on ski touring and snowshoeing.

Light Touring, Racing or Mountaineering In order to select the right equipment one should give some thought to what kind of ski touring is for him. For most it is light touring, casual day trips of short duration on easy trails. These people want a light, durable ski—but not the superlight skis of the racer. For those who combine touring and backpacking a tougher ski is needed to handle heavier loads in more rugged terrain. Sometimes these tourers have to consider snowshoes as part of their gear. And those who get into ski mountaineering and Alpine ski touring will require very sturdy skis with metal edges, safety-release bindings, and heavy boots to cope with the powder snow and Alpine slopes.

Rent or Buy While new ski tourers can outfit themselves with good skis, bindings, boots and poles for under $90 it may be wiser, in some cases, to rent equipment. This affords one the opportunity to try out different manufacturers, to evaluate the gear under the heavy wear and tear of rental conditions, and then choose those styles and design features that seem the most satisfactory. In many cases renting also saves the bother of transporting gear from home to site. Nearly all ski tour centers carry rental gear. Some also rent snowshoes. These are noted in the text.

Reference Books Several excellent books have been written about the how-to of ski touring. In lieu of instruction, studying one of these books is a good way to get started. While some of them emphasize the racing aspects of cross-country skiing, all of them contain useful information for the beginner and experienced alike. They are available in ski shops, sports stores, book stores and libraries. Many equipment catalogs also list these books:

> COMPLETE CROSS COUNTRY SKIING & SKI TOURING by Lederer & Wilson
> MANUAL OF SKI MOUNTAINEERING by Brower
> MOUNTAINEERING: THE FREEDOM OF THE HILLS, ed. Manning
> NEW CROSS COUNTRY SKI BOOK by Caldwell
> NORDIC TOURING & CROSS COUNTRY SKIING by Brady
> SKI TOURING FOR THE BEGINNER by Rusin & Kjellstrom
> SKI TOURING by Osgood
> SKI WAXING BOOK by Brady
> THE PLEASURES OF CROSS COUNTRY SKIING by Lund
> WILDERNESS SKIING by Steck & Tejada-Flores
> WINTER HIKING AND CAMPING by Adirondack Mountain Club

SNOWSHOEING

In America the use of snowshoes preceded the ski; they were indigenous as was the canoe. Eskimos and Indians developed this means of winter travel to insure communication and access to much needed game. Snowshoe design varied by regions, each developed as an answer to particular conditions: the *bearpaw* for maneuverability, the *beavertail* for faster travel in open country, and the *Yukon* for powder and open hiking. Modifications to these basic designs continues.

Snowshoes are available in traditional wood with rawhide lacings, and the lighter plastic or aluminum models. At present the former are the most popular. Be sure to use the lighter, stretch resistant neoprene lacings and harnesses for longer wear.

Outfitting is not expensive. Other than comfortable footwear that will keep feet dry and warm (Korea boots are excellent items), the snowshoes and harness can be had for less than $40. Add to this a ski pole or ice axe with a removable ski pole basket and the outfit is complete.

A person in good health can snowshoe. No special lessons are needed; only practice. While snowshoers generally cannot cover the same distance as skiers, they do enjoy more freedom of movement. More terrain is accessible to them than to skiers; trips into rugged country can be planned. Herein lies its greatest appeal.

In this book snowshoeing areas are noted along with ski touring facilities. Generally these are ski-area based locations, not always the best places for snowshoeing. However, open to snowshoers and skiers are the numerous state and federal parks and forests. Just about any hiking trail is a route for snowshoers. A reference library of trail guides is of real help to snowshoers. See *Introduction to Foot Trails in America.* Snowshoers are always welcome at ski touring centers. Their routes parallel the tracks of ski tourers. Many club-organized ski tours include snowshoers.

For book of interest to the snowshoer check the following:
    MOUNTAINEERING: THE FREEDOM OF THE HILLS, ed. Manning
    PARADISE BELOW ZERO by Rutstrum
    SNOWSHOE HIKES by Prater
    THE SNOW SHOE BOOK by Osgood and Hurley
    WINTER HIKING AND CAMPING by Adirondack Mountain Club

WINTER HIKING

In the areas where the snow fall is marginal many hikers stay on the trails throughout winter. Others limit their snow hiking to late fall and early spring. Considered here is casual hiking, not to be confused with winter mountaineering and its ultimate tests of skills, endurance and courage.

A different set of conditions are experienced in winter hiking. While the snow fall may be minimal the temperatures can be below freezing. Proper clothing and gear are needed. Footwear is of prime importance, for invariably the trails are muddy, icy or thinly snow-covered. Wet feet are the usual result. Insulated footwear like the Korea boots, a double boot, or a rubber hunting boot is necessary. Crampons and an ice axe are necessary items in any gear list.

Many areas of the nation are suitable for winter outings. The southern Appalachians, the Ozarks, and Midwest forests, the western desert country and Pacific Coast range offer good winter hiking. Topo maps, forest maps and guide books used for summer hiking will double for winter hiking references.

Of interest to winter hikers are the following books:

> PARADISE BELOW ZERO by Rutstrum
> WINTER HIKING AND CAMPING by Adirondack Mountain Club
> WINTER WALKS by Darville and Marshall
> WINTER WALKS NEAR SEATTLE AND EVERETT by Marshall

ORGANIZATIONS

Numerous clubs and groups in our country are devoted to furthering skiing as a recreation and sport. The United States Ski Association and its regional divisions along with the National Ski Areas Association function in close cooperation. They sanction, sponsor and conduct national and international competitions for both Alpine and Nordic events. Their periodicals keep skiers aware of current news about skiing. And they continue to be the best means of maintaining communication between people who

(Photo by Eugene A. Radloff)
Vilas County Snowshoer, Wisconsin

are like-minded in their appreciation of the values gained from skiing. For information about these two organizations write:

U.S. Ski Association
1726 Champa Street
Denver, Colorado 80202

National Ski Areas Association
99 Park Avenue
New York, New York 10016

Ski Touring Councils   Within the U.S. Ski Association are several divisions of the Ski Touring Council. These councils conduct training sessions and tours for skiers, hikers and snowshoers. All of them are made up of people eager to assist new skiers. Your membership and participation will add strength to the skiing fraternity and enrich your own life.

Eastern Division
Ski Touring Council (associated with U.S.S.A.)
West Hill Road
Troy, Vermont 05868

Central Division
Ski Touring Committee
9916 - 3rd Avenue South
Bloomington, Minnesota 55402

Rocky Mountain Division
Ski Touring Committee
472 South Ingalls
Denver, Colorado 80226

Far West Ski Association
Ski Touring Committee
812 Howard Street
San Francisco, California 94103

Also add to these groups a number of hiking, mountaineering, canoeing and biking oriented clubs who, when winter comes, also turn to ski touring and snowshoeing for their winter activities.

SKIER CLASSIFICATIONS

The Ski Touring Council has developed classifications for skiers in order to conduct comprehensive workshops and reasonably grade their tours. These are broad categories, not always uniform from one area in our nation to another.

BEGINNERS are encouraged to attend workshops and take their training on gentle fields and meadows over short distances.

NOVICES are skiers who can ski under control with a good snowplow turn. They are able to safely descend trails of up to 10 percent grade.

INTERMEDIATES are experienced skiers who can negotiate most all trails. They have good control on descents of up to 20 percent grade.

EXPERTS are the hardy skiers who can take any trail at reasonable speeds and bushwack through rough country.

TRAIL MARKINGS

Trails for ski touring are marked in a variety of ways. Some use the Ski Touring Council's suggested red signs, while many areas have developed their own colors and designs. U.S. Forest Service signs show a skier at termini and direction changes. Others simply use colored strips of plastic tied to trees and branches, or rely on hiking trail blazes. Many trails are obvious in good weather when they are groomed and tracked.

Groomed trails in this book are generally trails that have been cleared and are maintained or brushed out each year. Some places track or pack their trails, usually the ski touring centers and the downhill areas with their heavy equipment.

In certain areas the National Ski Areas Association signs are used. These are the familiar markers used at downhill areas. Be familiar with them; and remember that these signs are relative to the terrain. What is *easiest* one place can be *more difficult* elsewhere.

EASIEST — ● (circle)

MORE DIFFICULT — ■ (square)

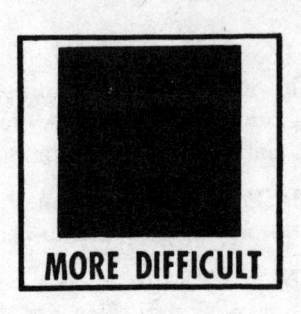

MOST DIFFICULT — ◆ (diamond)

CAUTION — ⚠ (exclamation in triangle)

Markers

SAFETY

Safety on snow trails is of prime consideration to all. Danger is inherent in any situation that finds a skier in severe weather, deep snow, touring over unfamiliar terrain, or underestimating the skills of the party and the time needed to complete the outing before dark. The Ski Touring Council has developed guidelines to help insure a safe trip.

1. Parties should consist of at least three.
2. Do not underestimate the time required. Deep snow and windfalls can slow progress to a fraction of a mile an hour.
3. Do not get overheated while climbing. Wear light clothing that can easily be opened.
4. Carry along at least one extra upper garment. Take a snack such as chocolate bars, dextrose tablets, candy, or a sandwich.

5. Take along a map and compass if you are not thoroughly familiar with the terrain. A pocket altimeter is also a useful instrument. Also take a spare aluminum or plastic ski tip, a cigarette lighter to make fire, a flashlight and a whistle to attract attention in case you get lost. A small sack will carry these miscellaneous items.
6. Before starting out, and on returning from a trip, advise the ski patrols if you are near a ski area, a ranger of a state or national park, a farmer or your friends.
7. If skins are to be used, be sure they fit. Adjust them before starting.
8. Watch for motorized vehicles.

The above are especially necessary safety measures for those outings that take skiers several miles from contact. It must be remembered that most areas do not have Ski Touring Patrols. With this in mind The Nordic Ski Touring Patrol suggests the following precautions.

1. Check your map as to proper route.
2. Check against a "check list" to see if you have all the necessary equipment.
3. Check your equipment. Tighten all screws, adjust bindings and inspect cables for breaks. Adjust climbing skins to your skis and look for worn straps.
4. Choose companions carefully; their ability will determine the extent of your tour. Always have at least four in your party.
5. Leave your trip schedule with a responsible person. Report your return.
6. Essentials to carry: easy on and off warm clothing for wind, cold and snow protection.
7. Have equipment to sustain life: waterproof matches, candle or fire starter, extra clothing, first aid kit, compass and map, 100-foot light rope, flashlight, plastic tarp, survival kit, ski repair kit, extra tip and ski wax.
8. On the trail, be self-sufficient. Set the pace to suit the least able member of the party. Keep warm with wool clothing and light windbreaker. Use layers of clothing. Avoid perspiration and conserve body heat; it is the essence of life.

9. Check your watch frequently with regard to distance to cover and unforeseen problems. Turning back before reaching objectives may take pleasure from the trip, but may save your life. Do not get caught in the dark.
10. Know about winter first aid, rescue, implementation and transportation.

For those who plan extensive trips a good knowledge of first aid and mountaineering medicine is essential. Survival gear must accompany every party. For excellent information on this subject contact The Mountaineering Rescue Council, Tacoma Unit, Box 696, Tacoma, Washington 98401. Ask for their list of books and aids.

It is always a good idea to phone ahead for a report on snow conditions in the area you plan to visit. A Saturday outing may have to be switched to Sunday, or a long drive for nothing can be avoided.

THE NEED FILLED BY THIS BOOK

At present many cross-country ski areas are coming into being, especially in eastern America. Ski clubs and hiking organizations are producing guides to touring areas and trails. The U.S. Forest Service, State Parks and local governments are also planning and distributing guides about trails in forests and cities. These are all local and regional in character. But there is a need for a book that covers snow trails in all parts of the nation; this book fills that need. To be sure, it does not describe every cross-country area in America. Rather it is a guide to selected places in easy-to-consult format.

Alpine and Nordic skiers alike will find these pages worthwhile. Ski tourers can use them to easily plan their next weekend outing near or away from home. Alpine skiers who have in the past restricted their time to the slopes can now enjoy a different skiing, either at their favorite downhill area or at a ski touring center. This text will familiarize skiers with the areas they plan to visit. In most cases supplemental maps, guides and references will enhance any trip. Names, addresses and prices or these are included in the text.

(Photo by Hubert Schriebl)
Good Form at Stratton Mountain

CHOOSING THE TRAILS

Ski tours are usually day outings of short mileage: anywhere from 2-3 miles for beginners, and up to 15-16 miles for experienced skiers. While there will always be ski touring and snowshoeing done in open country and local surroundings those new to ski touring will find it is convenient and comfortable to start a trip from a point where lodgings, parking and hot food are available. With this in mind ski touring areas are described here and more are mentioned. Most of these are associated with a ski touring center, ski shop, resort or downhill facility. Only a few areas are menaced by snowmobiles. The trails generally start from a place where accommodations are handy and the luxury of warming huts can be found along the way. This makes for good family touring. Many of the trails are suitable for children. Nearly all the trips are loop or return routes; therefore transportation is not a problem for traveling skiers.

Most of the trails listed here allow day use without charge, or at the most a nominal parking fee. All will appreciate your business at the snackbar and ski shop.

Instruction and guided tours are usually a part of these centers. No attempt is made here to quote rates for rentals and instruction; both vary considerably. Generally the best rates are found at the small, informal ski touring centers. A query letter or phone call will secure the latest information.

HOW TO USE THIS BOOK

In the text several recurring headings are used to familiarize the reader with the areas described and help him, within the scope of this book, to decide on a location for a ski tour or snowshoe outing. These headings, and the information they encompass, are as follows:

Season　The best time for snow.

Location　Approximate geographical site.

Access　Generally the most popular or easiest route to the area.

Transportation Services Scheduled bus, train and air service where they are close enough to be of help.

Accommodations Location of meals and lodgings in the area.

Medical Assistance Location of nearest clinic or hospital.

Winter Activities Activities other than skiing or snowshoeing.

Ski Touring Description of the facilities, instruction and rentals.

Snowshoeing As above.

Downhill Skiing As above. Where they appear, the initials N I and E are universally recognized by skiers as meaning Novice, Intermediate and Expert. Figures giving elevations in feet identify Vertical Drop by the initials VD, as commonly used in ski facility descriptive listings.

References Where to obtain other guides, maps and information that will help make a better outing.

REFERENCE MAPS AND GUIDES

Unless familiar with an area, one should not attempt snow travel without a map. Many maps are prepared by county, state and federal agencies. Some guides and maps are put together by clubs and organizations interested in summer and winter travel. Keep in mind that while trails shown on a map are easily discernible in summer, they may not be so in winter; especially in broad open areas. Noted landmarks are sometimes snow-covered, signs are often absent and blazes obscured.

Good maps to use are those prepared by the U.S. Geological Survey. Of interest to the ski tourer are the 7½ and 15 minute quadrangle series. However, these maps do not always have the latest trails shown on them. When used in conjunction with a more current club map or a guide book for Forest Service maps they are usually quite adequate. Some areas remain unmapped today. Index sheets showing the names and locations of these quadrangles in states west of the Mississippi River can be had free of charge by writing:

>Distribution Section
>Geological Survey
>Federal Center
>Denver, Colorado 80225

For states east of Mississippi River write:

>Distribution Section
>Geological Survey
>1200 South Eads Street
>Arlington, Virginia 22202

When ordering quadrangles be sure to specify name, series and state in which they are located. List maps alphabetically. Enclose 75 cents for each map.

PUBLICATIONS OF INTEREST

Several publications are available to the self-propelled outdoor enthusiast. Timely articles on the how-to and where-to of skiing, snowshoeing and winter hiking are included. A subscription will form an important part of a good reference library.

>**AMERICAN HIKER**
>2236 Mimosa Drive
>Houston, Texas 77019

>**BACKPACKER**
>28 West 44th Street
>New York, New York 10036

>**HIKING AND SKI TOURING**
>Box 7421
>Colorado Springs, Colorado 80918

>**SKI MAGAZINE**
>Box 2896
>Boulder, Colorado 80302

TRAIL CAMPING
P.O. Box 310
Canoga Park, California 91305

WILDERNESS CAMPING
1654 Central Avenue
Albany, New York 12205

ENJOYING AND PROTECTING SNOW TRAILS

Along with the many hours of enjoyment to be found on the snow trails there goes a responsibility to protect them. We *must* not litter and we *must* clean up after others as we go—and we *must* not hesitate to correct others guilty of littering! When choosing a spot for a lunch stop try to pick a place where others are not likely to stop during summer. The same is true of an overnight stop. And be sure to camp on snow rather than revealed ground.

We can no longer think of using wood fires in areas where the downed branches and trees are snow covered. Anything standing, dead or alive, must be left. A small stove is quite adequate for preparing any meal.

Sanitation is best handled by burning toilet paper. Latrine spots should be well away from water sources and any summer use trails or camps.

The above habits, along with respect for property and animal life, is already a way of life for most of us interested in the outdoor experience, summer or winter. For us to continue into the wilds, quietly and unnoticed, is the only way to go.

(Photo by Elizabeth Presnikoff)
Stowe Ski Touring Center, Vermont

CHAPTER 2

TRAILS EAST

IN THE EAST the development of ski touring and specialized facilities for ski tourers has become an important part of winter recreation for the millions who live here. Entire communities cater to the ski tourer, while more and more inns and lodges offer the informal atmosphere that complements the casual style of ski touring. Good snow conditions, easy access, and a long season allow these centers to provide the very best ski touring in America.

Anyone skiing in the east should get copies of the *Ski Touring Guide,* $1.75, Ski Touring Council, West Hill Road, Troy, Vermont 05868. Also ask for their schedule of tours and workshops, $1.75. This guide covers touring areas in Connecticut, Maine, Massachusetts, New Hampshire, New Jersey, New York, Pennsylvania, Vermont and West Virginia.

Also consider the *Ski Touring Guide to New England,* by Bass, $3.95, Eastern Mountain Sports, 1041 Commonwealth Avenue,

Boston, Massachusetts 02215. This is an extensive guide to Massachusetts, Maine, New Hampshire and Vermont.

Boston, Massachusetts is headquarters of the Appalachian Mountain Club, an organization vitally interested in the use and preservation of our natural resources. The Club is made up of eight chapters in Connecticut, Massachusetts, New Hampshire, New York, Pennsylvania and Rhode Island. Ski touring, snowshoeing, mountaineering and winter hiking are all important parts of their winter program that includes guided tours, overnight camping and mountain climbing. For more information about their activities write Appalachian Mountain Club, 5 Joy Street, Boston, Massachusetts 02108.

CONNECTICUT

In the way of challenging slopes Connecticut offers little for the downhill skier, but it is a grand place for ski tourers—novice and expert. Gentle terrain with open farmlands and wooded areas is easily found for those Sunday outings. Only an hour or two from New York, it is an ideal location for weekend skiing.

The State Forests have many miles of trails and open routes for the tourer and snowshoer. Be sure to pick a route that is free of snowmobile travel. For more information about these areas write Connecticut Department of Environmental Protection, State Office Building, Hartford, Connecticut 06115.

In February a number of Nordic events are held at Salisbury, including jumping and ski touring races.

Of interest to ski tourers and snowshoers is the *Connecticut Walk Book,* $4.50, a guide to 500 miles of foot trails in the state. Maps are included, many of these routes are suitable for skiing and snowshoeing. Write to Connecticut Forest and Park Association, P.O. Box 389, East Hartford, Connecticut 06108.

PEOPLES STATE FOREST

This is a forested area along the east bank of the West Branch Farmington River. The trails are short leading to scenic summits and overlooks. Some shelters and picnic areas.

Season December thru mid-March. Operates daily.

Location Northwestern Connecticut east of Winsted.

Access State 8 and U.S. 44 bring traffic to Winsted. East of Winsted State 318 leaves U.S. 44 for Pleasant Valley. Cross Farmington River and take East River Road to Forest Headquarters and parking nearby.

Transportation Services Bus to Winsted; car rentals.

Accommodations Food and lodgings in Winsted and New Hartford.

Medical Assistance Winsted.

Ski Touring There is ample parking across from the Forest Headquarters. The surrounding fields are excellent for instruction purposes and practice. About 10 miles of trails are available along with unplowed roads. Topo maps will be needed to help determine which trails are suited to your skills. Sections of the forest are open and park-like. Skiers may find that making their own trails is best.

Snowshoeing This terrain is perhaps better suited to the snowshoer. They will certainly have more freedom of choice in routes leading to the modest summits in the forest.

References Write for trail map, Peoples State Forest, Pleasant Valley, Connecticut 06063. For snow conditions telephone (203) 329-2463 or 329-2530.

7½′ quadrangles: New Hartford, Winsted.

POWDER RIDGE SKI AREA

A downhill ski area featuring the usual amenities found at a good resort. A family oriented operation with attractive facilities. Only an hour or so from New York.

Season December thru March. Operates daily and nights.

Location South-central Connecticut south of Meriden.

Access I-91 brings traffic to the area. State 147 reaches Powder Hill Road and on to Powder Ridge Ski area.

Transportation Services Bus and trains to Meriden; car rentals. Free bus from Meriden to ski area for Inn guests.

Accommodations Food and lodging at the site. Nursery in Littiput Lodge.

Medical Assistance Meriden.

Winter Activities There is an area here for tobogganing and sledding. Ice skating also.

Ski Touring Using the lifts, ski tourers can gain the summit and the start of an Intermediate 3-mile trail. The trail is groomed. Complete sales, rentals and instruction.

Downhill Skiing 8 lifts service 13 trails and slopes for NIE. 450' base el.; 500' VD. Ski Patrol. Snowmaking. Complete sales, rentals and instruction.

MAINE

While not having a large number of organized ski touring centers or downhill areas, Maine does have the snow and terrain for good winter fun. A land of frozen lakes and forests makes this ideal for ski touring and snowshoeing.

ACADIA NATIONAL PARK

This is a small park in comparison with other national parks, but it is unique. Situated on an island, it is surrounded by the sea. Mountains and cliffs, lakes and rushing streams, forested hills and pastoral valleys are all part of this scene. Once snow-covered, wonderful winter activities can be planned here. The facilities are good and the scenery outstanding.

Season December thru April.

Location On the coast southeast of Bangor.

Tour Start at Sugarloaf/USA

Access I-95 brings traffic to the area. U.S. 1 and State 3 lead to the Park.

Transportation Services Airlines to Bangor; car rentals. Bus to Bar Harbor.

Accommodations Food and lodgings at Bar Harbor and Southwest Harbor. Snow camping in the Park, 6 miles south of Bar Harbor on State 3; no water.

Medical Assistance Bar Harbor.

Ski Touring At present the ski touring trails follow a network of carriage roads on Mt. Desert Island in the vicinity of Sargent and Penobscot Mountains. These trails are separate from snowmobile routes, and offer a wide variety of outings with many short loops. About 40 miles of trails, most of them suitable for novices and intermediates. The trails are signed. No instruction or rentals in the area.

Snowshoeing This is great country for snowshoeing. Modest peaks can be ascended; Mt. Cadillac is the tallest at 1,530 feet. Dense forest, open meadows, and hillsides with grand vistas of the sea promise to make any snowshoe trip memorable. No rentals.

References Superintendent, Acadia National Park, Hulls Cove, Maine 04644. Tel. (207) 288-3338. Ask for topo map of *Acadia National Park*, $1.50. Also get *Phillips Trail Map*, $1.05 postpaid.

AKERS SKI

Akers Ski is the hub for things going on in this valley surrounded by mountains. Here is a wonderful setting for ski touring on trails suitable for novice and experts. Grand views from some of these routes.

Season December thru March. Operates daily.

Location Western Maine above Rumford.

Access U.S. 2 brings traffic to the area. State 5 and 120 reach Andover.

Transportation Services Bus to Rumford.

Accommodations Motels in Rumford. Food in Andover.

Medical Assistance Rumford.

Ski Touring Akers Ski is a touring center for the trails around Andover. Skiers here are very active in racing programs as well as touring. Use of Akers Ski Shop is on an informal basis. You may park your car here and take to the trails from this point. Leading from the shop is a 6-mile trail marked and tracked. Intermediate and expert. Beginners can use part of the trail. Map available at the shop. At Akers are complete sales and rentals. No instruction, but plenty of help.

There are also many other trails in the Andover area. Ask about them at Akers Ski. Or consult the Ski Touring Council's guidebook.

References   Akers Ski, Andover, Maine 04216. Tel. (207) 392-4582.

15' quadrangles: Rumford, Old Speck Mtn.

THE CROSS COUNTRY SKI PLACE

This shop is headquarters for ski touring in this part of Maine's rugged coastal country. The services here are specialized: touring only for adults and children. Informal and personal assistance from the proprietor.

Season   November thru March. Mostly afternoon hours; shop closed on Mondays.

Location   On southwestern Maine coast between Bath and Wiscasset.

Access   U.S. 1 brings traffic to Montsweag Road and The Cross Country Ski Place.

Transportation Services   Bus to Bath and Wiscasset; car rental in Bath.

Accommodations   Food and lodgings nearby on U.S. 1.

Medical Assistance   Bath.

Ski Touring   Over 5 miles of trails are available free here for Intermediates. More trail locations for all classes upon request. Complete sales and rentals; some second-hand equipment. Also free instruction and waxing advice on the premises.

References   The Cross Country Ski Place, Monstweag Road, Woolwich, Maine. Mailing address: RFD 3, Wiscasset, Maine 04578. Tel. (207) 443-5878 and 822-7637.

SQUAW MOUNTAIN

A big resort in north-central Maine. Ski-In Motel and all the amenities. They have a ski touring program operating daily, December thru April. 20 miles of groomed and signed trails for N-3, I-5, E-4. Complete sales, rentals and instruction. During ski-week vacations Alpine skiers are encouraged to try ski touring at no cost; equipment and instruction free. Annual Squaw Mountain Ramble, a ski touring festival, includes 10 km race, 50 km tour and other events. Write Squaw Mountain, Greenville, Maine 04441.

SUGARLOAF/USA

Sugarloaf/USA is one of the top ski areas in the nation. Few places equal it for length of season and trails, consistently good snow, and fine accommodations.

Season December thru April. Operates daily and nights.

Location Western Maine west of Carrabassett.

Access I-95 and State 4 and 27 bring traffic north to the area.

Transportation Services Airlines to Augusta, Bangor and Waterville; car rentals.

Accommodations Food and lodgings at the site or Kingfield and Stratton. Nursery at the site.

Medical Assistance Kingfield and Farmington.

Ski Touring Trails here on mountain sides and at river banks, through stands of timber and across open fields. About 26 miles of marked and groomed trails for the Novice and Intermediate. Easily planned day tours. Complete sales, rentals and instruction.

Downhill Skiing 9 lifts service 23 slopes and trails. 36 miles for NIE. 4237' base el.; 2637 VD. Base and summit lodge. Complete sales, rentals and instruction.

References Sugarloaf Area Association, Kingfield, Maine 04947. Tel. (207) 237-2861.

15' quadrangle: Stratton

Touring at Squaw Mountain

MARYLAND

Touring in the state forests of western Maryland is becoming popular west of Cumberland. The snow is adequate and the terrain very suitable. However, at present designated trails are few.

NEW GERMANY STATE PARK

This park is in the Savage River State Forest, an area made up of some of Maryland's most rugged and beautiful country. Base elevation is under 1,500 feet while St. John Rock nears 3,000 feet. Hardwood forests and evergreens, open slopes and valleys with good vistas, all help make this good snow travel country.

Season   December thru March.

Location   Extreme western Maryland west of Cumberland.

Access   U.S. 40 reaches Grantsville. New Germany Road leads south to Park.

Transportation Services   Bus to Grantsville. Lodgings in Frostburg and Cumberland.

Medical Assistance   Frostburg.

Ski Touring   About 15 miles of trails have been laid out here. 3 loops, varying from 3-6 miles, begin and end at the Park. Existing woods roads and trails are used, suitable for Novices. Park recreation building is a warming hut, operating daily in season; advance notice required for use of recreation building. Telephone Park Superintendent (301) 895-5453.

Snowshoeing   There are roads and trails enough here and in other parts of the State Forest to satisfy the most experienced snowshoer. Meadow Mountain offers some good views of the countryside. Snowshoers are welcome alongside the new touring trails.

References   Write for a brochure of the *Savage River State Forest,* Department of Forests and Parks, P.O. Box 3278, LaVale, Maryland 21502.

7½' quadrangles: Avilton, Grantsville

(Photo by Frank B. Lawson, Jr.)
Savage River State Forest

MASSACHUSETTS

There are better than three dozen designated ski touring areas throughout this state, most of them free of snowmobiles. Many of these are short routes ideal for an afternoon or evening outing. Trails can be taken through urban parks, around reservoirs and golf courses, or into sanctuaries and small, wooded reservations. The urban areas often double as walking routes for strollers. Some areas are lighted for night touring. Nearly all are suitable for Novices and a few charge a nominal parking fee.

GRANVILLE STATE FOREST

This is very hilly country southeast of the Berkshires. Hubbard River courses through the forest, once the hunting grounds of the Tunxis Indians. A beautiful setting for summer camping and picnicking. During winter the foot trails can be used for touring and snowshoeing. The West Hartland Road through the forest is plowed. There is parking and winter camping here.

Season   December thru March. Operates daily.

Location   Southwestern Massachusetts on its border with Connecticut.

Access   I-95 brings traffic to the area. State 57 leads to the Forest entrance which is about 2 miles east of Tolland.

Transportation Services   None.

Accommodations   None.

Medical Assistance   Winsted, Connecticut.

Ski Touring   Several miles of trails available to skiers. Some of the trails join with those in the Tunxis State Forest in Connecticut. Most of these trails are limited to Intermediate and Expert. Trails are marked but not groomed for skiing. Good wildlife sightings possible here. Snowmobiles use the area also, but it is possible to get away from them, especially on snowshoes. Topo maps are a must to determine the type of trail for you.

References   Write for map-brochure of Granville State Forest, Granville, Massachusetts 10134. Tel. (413) 357-6611.
  7½' quadrangles: West Granville, Tolland Center

HARTWELL HILL SKI AREA

This is a small family operation, one born out of a man's desire to provide skiing facilities for his family. The setting is wooded in a suburban area.

Season   Mid-December thru mid-March. Operates weekends and holidays.

Location Northeastern Massachusetts, southwest of Lowell in Littleton.

Access I-495 brings traffic to the area. Exit Littleton on State 2A/110. Head west and make sharp right just over the bridge. Look for signs and follow Hartwell Road to Ski Area.

Transportation Services Bus to Littleton; car rentals.

Accommodations Snackbar at Lodge. Food and lodgings in Littleton.

Medical Assistance Emerson.

Ski Touring There are about 7 miles of old roads here suitable for Novice and Intermediates. The trails are kept cleared. Instruction and rentals available.

Snowshoeing Snowshoers use the same routes. Rentals are available at the Lodge.

Downhill Skiing This is not a big hill, but many enjoyable hours can be spent here. No crowded tow lines for the 6 slopes and trails rated NIE. Ski Patrol in attendance. Instruction and rentals available.

References Hartwell Hill Ski Area, Littleton, Massachusetts 01450. Tel. (617) 486-4546.

JUG END RESORT

As a resort Jug End leaves little to be desired. It is a complete year-round operation with the very best of everything in accommodations. The Berkshires are the setting for this very lovely vacation spot.

Season December thru March. Operates daily.

Location Extreme southwestern Massachusetts.

Access I-87 and I-90 bring traffic to the area. U.S. 7 reaches Great Barrington.

Transportation Services Bus and airlines to Great Barrington; car rentals.

Accommodations Food and lodgings at Jug End Resort.

Medical Assistance Great Barrington.

Winter Activities Indoor swimming pool and tennis courts. Ice skating and tobogganing.

Ski Touring Jug End has about 6 miles of groomed and signed touring trails suitable for all classes. There are instruction and rentals on the premises.

Snowshoeing Follow the same trails as the ski tourers. Rentals available here also.

Downhill Skiing On the premises and nearby at Catamount and Butternut. T-bar, snowmaking, sales, rentals and instruction.

References Jug End, South Egremont, Massachusetts 01258. Tel. (800) 292-5004.

PITTSFIELD STATE FOREST

In the heart of the Berkshires this is an excellent ski touring area. There is ample parking and a warming hut. Shelters and picnic areas will be found along some of the trails. Snowmobiles have their own trails, shared with hikers.

Season December thru March. Operates daily.

Location Western Massachusetts west of Pittsfield.

Access I-87, Taconic Parkway, and I-90 bring traffic to the area. U.S. 7 and 20 reach Pittsfield. To get to the forest leave downtown Pittsfield via West Street, go under the RR bridge west to Churchill Street, north to Cascade, west to the forest.

Transportation Services Airlines and buses to Pittsfield; car rentals.

Accommodations Food and lodging in Pittsfield.

Medical Assistance Pittsfield.

Ski Touring The Taconic Skyline Trail forms the backbone of this system designed with skiers in mind. There are about 15 miles of trails suitable for all classes. Using established foot trails skiers can take outings from under a mile to 3½ miles. Loop outings up to 10 miles can be planned by connecting these trails. There are some short trails for practicing fast downhill runs. Trails are signed and maintained. There is a terrific downhill run for Experts on the Berry Pond Circuit Road—if you can make it to Berry Hill (2200) and are willing to put up with the snowmobiles. Maybe in the middle of the week is best for this.

Snowshoeing Some of the steeper trails are just right for snowshoers. Wonderful vistas for those who reach Berry Hill on a clear day. Use the Turner Trail and miss the snowmobile traffic.

References A very complete map is available from the Pittsfield State Forest, Pittsfield, Massachusetts 01201. Tel. (413) 442-8992. This map lists the trails, their difficulty and length.

7½' quadrangles: Hancock, Pittsfield West

WAUBEEKA SPRING

A golf course is used for a good portion of the touring trails here. This is another North American Nordic affiliate. Lots of help and good instruction.

Season December thru March; operates daily.

Location Extreme northwest Massachusetts, south of Williamstown.

Access U.S. 7 and State 43 reach Waubeeka Spring.

Transportation Services Bus and airlines to Pittsfield; car rentals.

Accommodations Food and lodgings nearby.

Medical Assistance Williamstown.

62 • TRAILS EAST

Ski Touring 10 miles of groomed and marked trails for NIE. Complete sales, rentals and instruction.

Reference Waubeeka Spring Ski Touring Center, Waubeeka Country Club, Williamstown, Massachusetts 02167. Tel. (413) 458-3000.

WYCKOFF PARK SKI TOURING CENTER

As a member of the North American Nordic Ski Touring System this place offers very complete facilities for the ski tourer. The trails have been laid out on the golf course and through the surrounding woods. Close to population centers. Mt. Tom Ski Area is connected to the center by a touring trail.

Season Mid-December thru mid-March. Operates daily.

Location South-central Massachusetts in Holyoke.

Access I-91 brings traffic to Holyoke. Exit 17 to State 141 and go 1 mile north to the Wyckoff Park Ski Touring Center.

Transportation Services Bus to Holyoke; car rentals.

Accommodations Food and lodgings in Holyoke.

Medical Assistance Holyoke.

Ski Touring Over 15 miles of trails, some groomed and signed for NIE. Guided tours for Beginners and Experts. Complete sales, rentals and instruction; housewives weekday special. Races on Sunday. Nominal day-use fee. Free trail use when renting or buying at Center.

References Wyckoff Park Ski Touring Center, Route 141, Holyoke, Massachusetts 01040. Tel. (413) 532-7805.

NEW JERSEY

While New Jersey has the terrain and snow conditions for touring in certain areas, little has been done to develop ski touring. The state forests and parks offer the best opportunities, using established trails and unplowed roads.

STOKES STATE FOREST

The Appalachian Trail passes through Stokes State Forest along the ridge of the Kittatinny Mountains. Some wonderful views from these heights.

Season   December thru March. Operates daily.

Location   Northwest New Jersey above Branchville.

Access   U.S. 206 passes through the Forest.

Transportation Services   None.

Accommodations   Food and lodgings along U.S. 206.

Medical Assistance   Newton.

Winter Activities   While there are no downhill facilities here, there are areas for sledding. Ice skating is done on Lake Ocquittunk. Ice fishing is also popular in the Park and surrounding areas. Winter camping is permitted at Shotwell Campground on a do-it-yourself basis. No running water.

Ski Touring   A section of the Park has been set aside for the express use of skiers and snowshoers. About 10 miles of trails are available for Novice, Intermediate and Expert. A topo map will be handy in matching trails to your skills. There are some excellent Intermediate and Expert runs. The trails follow logging roads, fire accesses and old footpaths. There is parking at trail heads.

There are no instruction or rentals. Check in at the Park headquarters for latest information on trail conditions.

Snowshoeing   Same trails and routes for snowshoers. Appalachian Trail shelters are accessible to snowshoers.

References   Write for winter facilities map, Stokes State Forest, RD, Branchville, New Jersey 07826. Tel. (201) 948-3820.

NEW HAMPSHIRE

The White Mountains, snow-covered meadows, quiet woods, and trails along old logging roads are all part of the scene for ski

(Photo by Elizabeth Presnikoff)
Telemark Turns at Stowe

touring here in New Hampshire. Good snow conditions and a long season are the rule. Add to the above a closeness to population centers, and it's little wonder so many people head for New Hampshire ski touring centers on weekends and holidays.

The facilities are numerous and extensive. Jackson is the first town in America devoted to ski touring. Throughout the state workshops, instruction, races and tours are conducted regularly by ski areas, inns and resorts, clubs and various organizations. There are few winter weekends when some sort of touring activity is not being held.

THE BALSAMS—WILDERNESS SKI AREA

A very complete resort billed as the "Switzerland of America." The northern White Mountains are the setting for skiing at nearby Wilderness Ski Area.

Season Mid-December thru mid-April. Operates daily.

Location Northern New Hampshire at Dixville Notch.

Access I-93 brings traffic north. U.S. 3 leads further north to State 26 and Dixville Notch.

Transportation Services Bus service to Colebrook, west of Dixville Notch.

Accommodations Food and lodgings at the Balsams; baby sitting service and movie theater. Base lodge at Wilderness Ski Area; cafeteria and snack bar.

Medical Assistance Hospital within 10 miles.

Winter Activities Ice skating, sledding and tobogganing, sleigh rides.

Ski Touring At the Wilderness Ski Area there are 15 miles of groomed and mostly signed trails suitable for NIE. Generally better snow here than many areas further south. Instruction, sales and rentals at base lodge.

Snowshoeing The same trails can be used, or the more adventuresome can strike out on their own. Rentals are available.

Downhill Skiing 3 lifts service 12 trails. NIE. Ski Patrol. Complete sales, rentals and instruction.

Reference The Balsams, Dixville Notch, New Hampshire 03578. Tel. (603) 255-3400. Wilderness Ski Area, Tel. (603) 255-3951.

15' quadrangle: Dixville

DARTMOUTH OUTING CLUB

One of the nation's oldest outing clubs, the D.O.C. maintains a 70-mile section of the Appalachian Trail along with another 50 miles in the general vicinity. Many miles are suitable for ski touring and snowshoeing in the area between Woodstock, Vermont (Green Mountains) to Warren, New Hampshire and the White Mountains.

Write for a map and descriptive information, 25 cents, Dartmouth Outing Club, P.O. Box 9, Hanover, New Hampshire 03755.

FRANCONIA INN

Catering to the ski tourer and snowshoer the Franconia Inn is a member center of the North American Nordic Ski Touring System. This is a very complete, yet informal establishment, in the heart of the White Mountains. Also an excellent location for the Alpine ski areas in the region: Mittersill Mountain and Cannon Mountain.

Season Mid-November thru mid-April. Operates daily.

Location Northwest New Hampshire, south of Littleton.

Access I-91 and I-93 bring traffic to the area. State 116 reaches Franconia Inn.

Transportation Services Bus to Littleton; car rentals.

Accommodations Food and lodgings at Franconia Inn.

Medical Assistance   Littleton.

Ski Touring   Touring can begin and end here with miles of trails groomed and signed for NIE. Most of these are Forest Service and AMC hiking trails. Complete sales and rentals; waxing. Instruction and guided tours. Also winter camping and backpacking.

Snowshoeing   Snowshoers are welcome here, with some of the hiking trails better suited to snowshoes. Rentals available in Franconia.

Reference   Franconia Inn, Route 116. Franconia, New Hampshire 03580. Tel. (603) 823-8896.

15' quadrangle: Moosilauke

FRANCONIA NOTCH STATE PARK

Spectacular scenery and good snow conditions provide great touring here. South of the Park are several Alpine ski areas.

Season   December thru mid-April. Operates daily.

Location   Northwest New Hampshire, south of Littleton.

Access   I-93 brings traffic to the area.

Transportation Services   Bus to Franconia and Littleton; car rentals.

Accommodations   Food and lodgings in the area and nearby Franconia and Littleton.

Medical Assistance   Littleton.

Ski Touring   There is a 5-mile trail system here, groomed and color-marked. The longest trail is over 2 miles, with others looping off it; Novice and Intermediate. Instruction and rentals available at the Peabody Slopes Building near the Echo Lake parking lot. Tours can be one way to another parking lot reached via. U.S. 3/I-93.

References   Write for *Ski Touring Trail Map,* Franconia Notch State Park, Franconia, New Hampshire 03580.

15' quadrangle: Franconia

GRAY LEDGES

Gray Ledges is a Christian conference and retreat, an interdenominational center where all are welcome. This 200-year-old farmstead is on 1,300 acres of beautiful mountain scenery; an ideal touring center for those who need only the necessities and like quiet and good fellowship. Close by are Alpine ski areas.

Season   January thru March.

Location   Western New Hampshire in Grantham, just north of Claremont.

Access   I-93/89 bring traffic to the area. State 110 reaches Grantham.

Transportation Services   Bus to Claremont; car rentals.

Accommodations   Lodgings at Gray Ledges. Snack shop; bring your own food.

Medical Assistance   Hanover.

Winter Activities   Hiking, sledding and tobogganing.

Ski Touring   There are 5 miles of marked trails here for Novices and Intermediates. Some rentals. Instruction by appointment. Picnic lunches and guided tours. Snack shop. Nominal parking and trail usage fee. Mountaintop Ski Club membership provides unlimited use of touring trails for a nominal fee.

Snowshoeing   Plenty of room here in the woods and over open fields. Follow the touring trails, or do it on your own. Some rentals.

Reference   Gray Ledges, Grantham, New Hampshire 03753. Tel. (603) 863-9880.
   15' quadrangle: Sunapee

JACKSON

In the winter the entire community of Jackson is devoted to ski touring. The Jackson Ski Touring Foundation with its member Alpine ski areas, inns, shops and commercial establishments, have worked to provide the very finest in facilities for the tourer and snowshoer. This is a unique approach that offers the tourer a variety of trails, lodgings and amenities. This is America's first ski touring village.

Season December thru April.

Location Northeast New Hampshire above North Conway.

Access State 16 reaches Jackson.

Transportation Services Bus to North Conway and Jackson. Car rentals in North Conway. Shuttle bus from North Conway to Jackson, connecting the Jackson Ski Touring Foundation member inns with the downhill ski areas at Black Mountain, Tyrol and Wildcat Mountain.

Accommodations Food and lodgings at the 9 member inns, including rentals, instruction, waxing rooms, direct access to the trails surrounding the Jackson area, and the convenience of shuttle bus service at their doors. Most offer baby sitting services.

Medical Assistance North Conway.

Winter Activities Ice skating on the Jackson Village pond. Sledding, tobogganing and skating at some of the inns.

Ski Touring Over 70 miles of trails here in the upper Mt. Washington Valley. 30 trails rated for NIE, all maintained to a varying degree and marked. The trail system connects 9 member inns with Jackson and 3 member downhill areas: Black Mountain, Tyrol and Wildcat Mountain, offering single lift tickets for the summit trails that lead back down to Jackson. Besides instruction, sales and rentals at most of the above 12 places, they are also to be had in Jackson at the Ski Touring Center. Guided tours, maps and lots of help here also. A nominal fee or club membership is required of trail users. Inn guests have use of all trails.

Snowshoeing The same routes are open to snowshoers, plus a variety of more difficult climbs. Rentals available in Jackson.

Reference Jackson Ski Touring Foundation, Jackson, New Hampshire 03846. Tel. (603) 383-9355. Contact these people for help in making reservations and learning more about ski touring in the Jackson area.

15' quadrangle: North Conway.

LOON MOUNTAIN

This is another White Mountains downhill area, but one that promises limited lift lines. All of the extras here, including a narrow-gauge railroad ride from parking lot to slopes.

Season   Thanksgiving thru Easter. Operates daily.

Location   North-central New Hampshire, east of Lincoln.

Access   I-93 brings traffic to Exit 30 and Lincoln. State 112 (Kancamagus Highway) leads east to Loon Mountain.

Transportation Services   Bus to North Woodstock.

Accommodations   Food and lodgings at site. Nursery.

Medical Assistance   Littleton and Conway. Clinic nearby.

Winter Activities   Ice skating and tobogganing.

Ski Touring   Over 17 miles of signed trails for NIE. 5 miles are groomed. Complete sales, rentals and instruction.

Downhill Skiing   4 lifts service 17 trails for NIE. 1000' base el.; 1800' VD. Complete sales, rentals and instruction.

Reference   Loon Mountain, Lincoln, New Hampshire 03251. Tel. (603) 745-8111.

15' quadrangle: Franconia

PINKHAM NOTCH CAMP

This facility is operated by the Appalachian Mountain Club. In the shadow of Mt. Washington this area offers some of America's finest touring. A long season and excellent snow conditions are always expected.

Season   Mid-November thru April.

Location   Northeast New Hampshire above Jackson.

(Photo by Larry Cox, Loon Mountain News Bureau)
Trail from Loon Mountain

Access State 16 reaches Pinkham Notch Camp.

Transportation Services Bus to North Conway. Shuttle bus from North Conway to Jackson to Pinkham Notch Camp and other skiing spots in the area.

Accommodations Food and lodgings at Pinkham Notch Camp and Jackson. Wildcat Ski Area, with complete facilities, is within walking distance. Zealand Notch cabin open all winter.

Medical Assistance North Conway.

Winter Activities Winter mountaineering, ice climbing, skating.

Ski Touring About 15 miles of touring trails in the immediate area. They are signed and color-marked for degree of difficulty. Something here for NIE. Rentals available.

Snowshoeing Touring trails are open to snowshoers. Forest trails that are too tough for ski touring will allow snowshoers to move up to some very beautiful vistas.

Downhill Skiing Spring Alpine skiing at Tuckerman Ravine, reached by hiking/skiing from Pinkham Notch Camp; March thru June. Shelter, snacks and light lunches. Leantos and camping.

Reference Pinkham Notch Camp, Gorham, New Hampshire 03581. Tel. (603) 466-3994.

15' quadrangles: Mt. Washington, Gorham, Crawford Notch, North Conway.

TEMPLE MOUNTAIN SKI AREA

Close as it is to the population centers of New Hampshire and Massachusetts, Temple Mountain is a popular ski area. A high base elevation (1486') insures a long season of good snow conditions.

Season December thru April. Operates daily.

Location Southern New Hampshire, east of Peterborough on State 101.

Access U.S. 202 reaches Peterborough.

Transportation Services Bus to Peterborough; car rentals. Airlines to Keene and Manchester; car rentals.

Accommodations Food at base lodge; nursery. Lodgings in Peterborough.

Medical Assistance Peterborough.

Winter Activities Sledding and tobogganing at Miller State Park across from Temple Mountain Ski Area.

Ski Touring There are excellent facilities here for ski tourers. Instruction, sales and rentals are available, along with guided tours and winter camping outings. Touring lessons are also given 2 nights a week. Lifts can be used to reach some of the trails.

The backbone of the trail system is the Wapack Trail, a skyline route following the ridge of the Wapack Range for about 21 miles. From Temple Mountain ski area it stretches north 7 miles and 14 miles south. In all about 35 miles of marked touring trails. NIE can be accommodated here on looping trails from one to 10 miles in length. The trails are maintained, providing comfortable use.

Snowshoeing Snowshoers use the same scenic trails, or take out on their own through the forest. Rentals available.

Downhill Skiing 6 lifts service 12 slopes and trails rated NIE. 600'VD. Complete sales, rentals and instruction.

15' quadrangle: Peterborough

WATERVILLE VALLEY

Another very complete Alpine ski area that has developed a comprehensive ski touring program. A variety of vacation packages are available. The skiing is the best, the season longer than many other downhill areas.

Season December thru April. Operates daily.

Location North-central New Hampshire above Plymouth.

Access I-93 brings traffic to State 49 and Waterville Valley.

Transportation Services Bus to Plymouth. Car rentals in Waterville Valley. Free shuttle bus from ski areas to lodges.

Accommodations Food and lodgings in Waterville Valley. Nursery.

Medical Assistance Plymouth.

Ski Touring There are about 35 miles of groomed and signed trails here for NIE—woods, open fields and alongside the Mad River. Guided tours, picnic lunches, moonlight tours. Instruction for adults and children. Touring vacation packages can be combined with Alpine skiing. Complete sales and rentals.

Snowshoeing All the touring trails and more are here for the snowshoer. No rentals.

Downhill Skiing 9 lifts service 30 slopes and trails. NIE. 1850' base el.; 2020' VD. Complete sales, rentals and instruction.

Reference Waterville Valley Associates, Waterville Valley, New Hampshire 03223. Tel. (603) 236-8371.
   15' quadrangle: Franconia

WINDBLOWN

This is another small ski touring center that is short on extras and amenities, but long on the very best in trails, instruction and help for beginners and experienced alike. Snow comes early and stays late here in the Monadnock Region. For those who like their touring in quiet surroundings without frills, this is the place.

Season December thru March. Operates daily.

Location Extreme southern New Hampshire in New Ipswich, west of Nashua.

Access I-91 and I-93 bring traffic to the area. Windblown is in New Ipswich, just south of State 123/124 junction.

Transportation Services Bus to Jaffrey and Peterborough on U.S. 202.

Accommodations At Windblown there are lodgings for 30-40 with sleeping bags. Very reasonable. Reservations are necessary. Some food items for sale. Pack in your own main meals. Children and pets are welcome.

Medical Assistance Peterborough.

Ski Touring Better than 11 miles of groomed and signed trails are here for NIE. Warming hut, hot drinks, indoor waxing. Shop with complete sales, rentals and instruction.

Snowshoeing Everything here is also for the snowshoers. Rentals available.

Reference Al Jenks, RFD, New Ipswich, New Hampshire 03071. Tel. (603) 878-2869.

15' quadrangle: Peterborough

NEW YORK

There are many developed ski touring areas in New York along with a great number of public lands and trails. The state forest system provides unlimited opportunities in the Adirondacks and Catskills. The Finger Lakes area in mid-New York offers good ski touring and some winter hiking.

For more about skiing on public lands see *Winter Hiking in the New York State Forest Preserve,* Department of Environmental Conservation, Albany, New York 12201. This booklet covers winter routes in the Adirondacks, Catskills, the Northville-Lake Placid Trail, Schroon Lake and Old Forge Regions, along with a mention of the trails in the Cranberry Lakes Region.

ADIRONDAK LOJ

The Loj provides one of the nation's finest ski touring centers. Organized ski touring in America probably got its start here back

(Photo by Garfield Jones)
Summit Touring in Adirondacks

around the turn of the century. Certainly it is one of the oldest and best developed in terms of trails well maintained and variation.

Season   December thru March. Operates daily.

Location   East-central New York, east of Lake Placid.

Access   I-87 brings traffic north to State 73, then west to Lake Placid and the Adirondak Loj.

Transportation Services   Bus to Lake Placid; car rentals. Airline to Saranac Lake; car rentals.

Accommodations   Food and lodgings at Adirondak Loj and Lake Placid. For winter camping contact Johns Brook Lodge,

Winter Camps, Box 52, Keene Valley, New York 12943. Tel. (518) 576-4302.

Medical Assistance   Lake Placid.

Winter Activities   This area is a winter sports center. Tobogganing and sledding at Lake Placid, along with ice skating—indoor and outdoor. Ice fishing on Lake Champlain, Saranac Lake and others in the area. At Van Hoevenburg there is an Olympic bobsled run.

Ski Touring   About 100 miles of trails for NIE. Trails lead to mountain peaks, across open valleys, meadows and frozen lakes, and through dense forests. Old logging roads, fire accesses and abandoned railbeds are all used by ski tourers. The largest portion of trail mileage is on the well developed and signed foot trails leading to the surrounding peaks. There are also specified ski touring trails, signed and maintained. One trail links the Loj with Mt. Van Hoevenburg Recreation Area Ski Touring Trails system with its extensive network for NIE.

At the Adirondak Loj there are rentals and instruction along with advice on trail choices. A trading post provides snacks. Other rentals are available at Ruthie's Run on Main Street in Lake Placid.

Snowshoeing   Snowshoers take to the same trails here. Their range is generally farther, with some peaks the goals of the more experienced snowshoers. Rentals at the Loj or at Ruthie's Run in Lake Placid.

Winter Camping and Mountaineering   Any number of possibilities exist here for snow camping. For the expert there is winter mountaineering. The Adirondack Mountain Club conducts a school in midwinter. Inquire at the Loj.

Reference   Adirondak Loj, Box 87, Lake Placid, New York 12946. Tel. (518) 523-3441. Ask for brochure about trails at Adirondak Loj and Mt. Van Hoevenburg Recreation Area.

15' quadrangle: Mt. Marcy.

BEAR MOUNTAIN STATE PARK

Palisades Interstate Park is a winter playground once the snow is deep enough. This area is a very scenic and complete winter resort, close enough to New York to be the favorite of thousands.

Season December thru March. Operates daily; some nights.

Location Southern New York along the Hudson River above New York City.

Access New York State Thruway and Palisades Interstate Parkway bring traffic to the area.

Transportation Services Bus to Bear Mountain Inn, other than January to third Sunday in February.

Accommodations Food and lodgings at Bear Mountain Inn. Food at Silver Mine Ski Area.

Medical Assistance Park first aid.

Winter Activities At Bear Mountain there are runs for sleds and toboggans. Skating is popular here, featured at night, weekends and holidays. Ski jumping is conducted next to the Inn. Some of the many lakes in Palisades Interstate Park are open to ice fishing. When the snow is marginal the foot trails throughout the park provide a unique experience.

Ski Touring 6 trails have been laid out and marked for ski touring, ranging from 2-6 miles in length. Recommended for Novice and Intermediates. They follow bridle paths, hiking trails and access roads. They rise and descend easy slopes, cross frozen marshes and skirt meadows and iced lakes. Vistas are wonderful. Extended tours and winter camping are possible with the use of topo and park maps. Sales, rentals and instruction at Silver Mine Ski Center.

Snowshoeing There are about 200 miles of foot trails in the park, most of them accessible to snowshoers. With topo maps in hand numerous loop hikes can be worked out, from a pleasant day trip to an overnighter.

Downhill Skiing 5 lifts service 3 slopes and trails for NIE. Night skiing. Base lodge with snacks. Complete sales, rentals and instruction.

Reference   Palisades Interstate Park, Bear Mountain, New York 10911. Tel. (914) ST6-2701. Ask for *Trail Map* and description sheets of trail data for ski touring, 50 cents postpaid.

7½' quadrangles: Peekskill, Popolpen Lake, Thiells

BARK EATER

An old family farm in Keene is home for this ski touring center, one of North American Nordic's affiliates. Home cooking, casual lodgings, and everything for the ski tourer are featured here.

Season   December thru March; operates daily.

Location   Northern New York east of Lake Placid in Keene.

Access   State 73 reaches Keene.

Transportation Services   Bus to Lake Placid; center meets bus. Car rentals in Lake Placid.

Accommodations   Food and lodgings at Bark Eater Lodge.

Medical Assistance   Keene Valley and Lake Placid.

Ski Touring   10 miles of groomed, tracked and signed trails for NIE. Complete sales, rentals and instruction. Also the ski touring trails of Mt. Marcy and Mt. Van Hoevenburg are close by. The center conducts guided tours, half days and full days.

Reference   Bark Eater Ski Touring Center, Alstead Mill Road, Keene, New York 12942. Tel. (518) 576-2221.

BIG TUPPER SKI AREA

This downhill ski area is located in the heart of the Adirondacks. It boasts good snow conditions and excellent touring country.

Season   Mid-December thru Easter. Operates daily.

Location   North-central New York below Lake Placid.

Access   I-87 brings traffic to the area. State 73 leads west to Tupper Lake and the ski center.

Transportation Services   Airlines to Saranac Lake; car rentals. Bus to Lake Placid; car rentals.

Accommodations   Food and lodgings at site.

Medical Assistance   Tupper Lake.

Ski Touring   7 miles of trails for NIE. Groomed and signed. Complete sales, rentals and instruction.

Downhill Skiing   3 lifts service 9 slopes and trails for NIE. Night skiing on Wednesday and Friday. 2000' base el.; 800' VD. Complete sales, rentals and instruction.

Reference   Big Tupper Ski Area, P.O. Box 820, Tupper Lake, New York 12896. Tel. (518) 359-3651.

15' quadrangle: Long Lake

ERIE BRIDGE CROSS COUNTRY SKI CENTER

Devoted to the ski tourer, this informal establishment is situated in the rolling apple country of mid-New York. Friendly help and advice for beginners.

Season   November thru April. Operates daily.

Location   Central New York, just south of Syracuse.

Access   I-81 brings traffic to Exit 13, west to U.S. 20 and Tully Farms.

Transportation Services   Bus to LaFayette or Syracuse. Car rentals in Syracuse.

Accommodations   Food and lodgings nearby.

Medical Assistance   LaFayette.

Ski Touring   About 10 miles of groomed trails for NIE. Free trails. Warm up area. Complete sales, rentals and instruction.

Reference Erie Bridge Cross Country Ski Center, P.O. Box 65, LaFayette, New York 13084. Tel. (315) 677-3637.

7½' quadrangle: Jamesville

FO'CASTLE FARMS

Fo'castle Farms is a large working orchard-farm that offers something more than their produce. A gift shop features homemade bread and pies. A small restaurant is part of this family establishment. A charming boutique is on the premises, just behind the restaurant terrace.

Season Mid-December thru March. Operates daily.

Location Mid-eastern New York above Schenectady in Burnt Hills.

Access I-87 and I-90 bring traffic to the area. State 50 reaches Burnt Hills.

Transportation Services Bus to Schenectady and airlines to Albany; car rentals.

Accommodations Food at the site. Food and lodgings in Burnt Hills.

Medical Assistance Schenectady.

Ski Touring A 5 mile trail has been located for some time and used by local residents and members of the two ski clubs in Burnt Hills. The trail starts at the Farm and moves through woods and open fields to reach fresh watercress in an open stream. The trail is blazed and suitable for Novices. The Farm's surrounding orchards are open to touring on gentle slopes. Instruction and rentals.

Snowshoeing Snowshoers are welcome here. No rentals.

Reference Fo'castle Farms, Burnt Hills, New York 12027. Tel. (518) 399-7801.

FROST RIDGE

This is a downhill ski area with new touring trails. Excellent for the beginner.

Season   December thru March. Operates daily; closed Monday.

Location   Western New York, southwest of Rochester in Le Roy.

Access   I-90 brings traffic to Exit 47, south on State 19 to North Road, then east to Conlon Road and the ski area.

Transportation Services   Airlines and buses to Rochester; car rentals.

Accommodations   Food and lodging in Le Roy. Food and winter camping at Frost Ridge.

Medical Assistance   Batavia.

Ski Touring   5 miles of groomed and signed trails for the Novice. Complete sales, rentals and instruction.

Downhill Skiing   4 lifts service 8 slopes and trails for NIE. 140' VD. Night skiing. Complete sales, rentals and instruction.

Reference   Frost Ridge, Inc., Conlon Road, Le Roy, New York 14482. Tel. (716) 967-9730.

7½' quadrangle: Le Roy

HAPPY VALLEY SKI CENTER

This downhill facility is operated by Alfred University Faculty-Student Association.

Season   December thru April. Operates daily; night skiing.

Location   Southwest New York, west of Hornell.

Access   State 244 reaches the ski area outside Alfred.

Transportation Services   Bus to Hornell; car rentals.

Accommodations   Base lodge with snacks. Food and lodgings nearby.

Medical Assistance   12 miles from site.

Ski Touring   Over 3 miles of groomed trails for Novices and Intermediates. Instruction and rentals.

Downhill Skiing   A lift and tow service 4 slopes and trails for NIE. 300' VD. Complete sales, rentals and instruction.

Reference   Happy Valley Ski Center, Faculty-Student Association, Alfred, New York 14802. Tel. (607) 587-8327.

INLET AND OLD FORGE

The ski touring center at Inlet conducts tours in conjunction with McCauley Mt. Ski Center.

Season   December thru March; operates daily.

Location   Northern New York

Access   State 28 reaches Inlet and Old Forge.

Trnasportation Services   None.

Accommodations   Food and lodgings in Inlet, Old Forge and Eagle Bay.

Medical Assistance   Old Forge.

Ski Touring   25 miles of groomed and signed trails for Novice and Intermediate. Trails lead out from McCauley Mtn. Ski Center, Inlet and Eagle Bay. A very extensive ski touring program here, with several guided tours each month. Complete instruction, sales and rentals at Inlet Ski Touring Center.

Reference   Write to Ski Touring Center, Inlet, New York 13360. Tel. (315) 357-3453.

MR. MOOSE OUTFITTERS

Ski touring here from December through March near Glenwood. 15 miles of signed and groomed trails. Complete sales, rentals and instruction. Snowshoe rentals. Food and lodgings at the site. For more information contact Mr. Moose outfitters, Box 108, Glenwood, New York 14069.

PINE RIDGE SKI AREA

A small downhill ski area by the southern edge of the Adirondack State Forest Preserve. It is mostly used by local families, but all are welcome.

Season   Mid-December thru mid-April. Operates on weekends.

Location   Central New York, north of Little Falls.

Access   I-90 brings traffic to the area to Little Falls. State 167 and 29 lead to Salisbury Center and east 3 miles on State 29A to Pine Ridge.

Transportation Services   None.

Accommodations   Snack bar at site. Lodgings nearby.

Medical Assistance   10 miles from Pine Ridge.

Ski Touring   Over 7 miles of trails have been cleared for NIE. They are marked, groomed and patrolled. Package tours on weekends include rentals, lunch, instruction and guide. Complete sales, rentals and instruction at ski shop.

Snowshoeing   Trails are open to snowshoers. No rentals.

Downhill Skiing   2 lifts service 7 slopes and trails. 150' VD. Sales, rentals and instruction.

Reference   Pine Ridge Recreation, Inc., 48 North Ann Street, Little Falls, New York 13365. Tel. (315) 429-9349.
   7½' quadrangles: Salisbury, Stratford

RUM RUNNER SKI TOURING CENTER

A member of the North American Nordic Ski Touring System. The Alp Horn Inn provides the amenities while the touring center is organized to meet all the needs of the ski tourer.

Season December thru March. Operates daily.

Location Northeast New York, above Glens Falls.

Access I-87 brings traffic north to Exit 25, then west on State 8 to Chestertown and Loon Lake.

Transportation Services Bus to Chestertown. Car rentals in Glens Falls.

Accommodations Food and lodgings at Alp Horn Inn.

Medical Assistance Glens Falls.

Ski Touring 10 miles of groomed and signed trails for NIE. Complete sales, rentals and instruction.

Reference Rum Runner Ski Touring Center, Alp Horn Inn, Loon Lake, New York 12951. Tel. (518) 494-3811.

SWAIN SKI CENTER

After being in business for over 25 years Swain continues to be a very popular ski area in western New York.

Season December thru mid-April. Operates daily.

Location West-central New York, northwest of Hornell.

Access State 408 reaches Swain.

Transportation Services None.

Accommodations Food at base lodge. Lodgings within 15 miles. Winter camping nearby.

Medical Assistance Hornell and Dansville.

Ski Touring 3 miles of groomed trails for the Novice. Also old logging roads. Complete sales, rentals and instruction. Guided tours.

Snowshoeing Snowshoers are welcome. No rentals.

Downhill Skiing 5 lifts service 23 slopes and trails for NIE.

Reference Swain Ski Center, Swain, New York 14884. Tel. (607) 545-9908.

7½′ quadrangle: Canaseraga

WEST MOUNTAIN

Eleven miles of slopes and trails here for the downhill skier. One of the East's biggest areas; limited lift lines. Mountain top touring trails.

Season December thru March. Operates daily; night skiing.

Location Eastern New York in Glens Falls.

Access I-87 brings traffic north to Exit 18, then west 2 miles to the ski area.

Transportation Services Bus and airlines to Glens Falls; car rentals.

Accommodations Food at the base lodge. Food and lodging in Glens Falls.

Medical Assistance Glens Falls.

Ski Touring About 5 miles atop the mountain for Intermediates and Experts. Lifts are needed to reach trails; free when you accompany a paying downhill skier. Trails are signed. Complete sales, rentals and instruction.

Downhill Skiing 6 lifts service 14 trails for NIE. 1010′ VD. Complete sales, rentals and instruction.

Reference West Mountain, Glens Falls, New York 12801. Tel. (518) 793-6606.

PENNSYLVANIA

While Pennsylvania has the terrain and snow conditions for good touring there are very few organized facilities or establishments for the ski tourer. The lack of suitable mountains for Alpine skiing has caused the skiing interest in Pennsylvania to lag behind other eastern states. Nevertheless good touring can be had on many sections of hiking trails in Pennsylvania forests. Allegheny National Forest has a well developed trail system (over 100 miles) including a section of the North Country Trail. The 85-mile loop of the Susquehannock Trial can be skied or snowshoed in part. The Black Forest Ski Touring Trail is a 7-mile loop designed for touring. See the *Ski Touring Guide*. The Baker Trail and Loyalsock Trail are other designated and signed routes for tourers and snowshoers.

CRYSTAL LAKE CAMP AND CONFERENCE CENTER

This informal camp caters year-round to group activities for schools and youth groups. Individuals are welcome to the facilities.

Season   December thru March. Operates daily.

Location   Northeastern Pennsylvania east of Williamsport.

Access   I-80 brings traffic to the area. U.S. 220 reaches to Hughesville, Picture Rocks and Tivoli. Watch for signs.

Transportation Services   Bus and airlines to Williamsport; car rentals.

Accommodations   Food and lodgings at site.

Medical Assistance   Muncy.

Winter Activities   There is a modest downhill area here. Also tobogganing and ice skating.

Ski Touring   10 miles of trails for Intermediates. Instruction and rentals available.

Snowshoeing   Snowshoers will find plenty of room to hike out on these 960 acres.

Reference   Crystal Lake Camp and Conference Center, R.D. 1, Hughesville, Pennsylvania 17737. Tel. (717) 584-2698.

   15' quadrangle: Eagles Mere

MOUNT AIRY LODGE

A complete winter resort in the Pocono Mountains.

Season   December thru March. Operates daily.

Location   Eastern Pennsylvania, southeast of Scranton at Mt. Pocono.

Accommodations   Food and lodgings at site. Health club, indoor pool.

Winter Activities   Sledding, tobogganing, ski-bob slope, ice skating, curling. Winter horseback riding.

Ski Touring   3½-mile trail groomed and signed for Novice and Intermediate. Complete sales, rentals and instruction.

Downhill Skiing   1 lift services 7 trails for NIE. Complete sales, rentals and instruction.

Reference   Mount Airy Lodge, Mount Pocono, Pennsylvania 18344. Tel. (717) 839-7133.

ELK MOUNTAIN SKI CENTER

A downhill ski area.

Season   December thru March. Operates daily; night skiing.

Location   Northeastern Pennsylvania, above Scranton and west of Uniondale.

Access   I-81 brings traffic to the area. U.S. 106 and State 107 lead to West Clifford and Uniondale respectively where county roads reach the site. Follow the signs.

Transportation Services   Bus and airlines to Scranton; car rentals.

Accommodations   Food at base lodge. Nursery.

Ski Touring   A 6-mile trail groomed and signed for Novice and Intermediate. Complete sales, rentals and instruction.

PENNSYLVANIA • 89

(Photo by Elizabeth Presnikoff)
Easy Does It

Reference Elk Mountain Ski Center, Uniondale, Pennsylvania 18470. Tel. (717) 679-2611.
7½' quadrangle: Clifford

SEVEN SPRINGS

Seven Springs boasts the largest base lodge in eastern United States. It is a complete year-round resort.

Season December thru February. Operates daily; night skiing.

Location Southwestern Pennsylvania east of Champion.

Access Pennsylvania Turnpike brings traffic to the area. Exit at Somerset to State 31 and follow signs.

Transportation Services None.

Accommodations Food and lodgings at site. Indoor pool, bowling alleys, game room, indoor miniature golf.

Medical Assistance At site.

Ski Touring 5 miles of groomed and signed trails. Complete sales, rentals and instruction.

Downhill Skiing 13 lifts services 14 slopes and trails for NIE. Complete sales, rentals and instruction.

Reference Seven Springs, Champion, Pennsylvania 15622. Tel. (814) 926-2031.

BLUE KNOB SKI AREA

Blue Knob is one of the biggest downhill areas in Pennsylvania, located in the Allegheny Mountains.

Season December thru March. Operates daily; night skiing.

Location West-central Pennsylvania south of Altoona near Pavia.

Access Pennsylvania Turnpike brings traffic to the area. U.S. 220 and State 869 lead to Blue Knob.

Transportation Services Bus to Altoona; car rentals.

Accommodations Food at base lodge; nursery. Food and lodgings in the area.

Medical Assistance Altoona.

Ski Touring 5-7 miles signed for NIE. 1000' VD. Complete sales, rentals and instruction.

Reference Blue Knob Ski Area, P.O. Box 184, Claysburg, Pennsylvania 16625. Tel. (814) 239-5111.

7½' quadrangle: Blue Knob

VERMONT

Vermont ski touring is unequaled anywhere in America. Mountain terrain, open valleys, forested slopes and a long season with good snow conditions provides ideal ski touring at some of the very best touring centers around. Also with its sister state, New Hampshire, Vermont has become the East's most popular area for ski touring. A wide selection of inns and lodges are currently catering to the ski tourer.

BLUEBERRY HILL FARM

A very informal and extremely pleasant ski touring center. Room and meals are taken in the main house. Dining is family style with the hosts at a long wooden table. Country cooking with elegance is the theme of this very charming inn. Everything here for the ski tourer.

Season Thanksgiving thru April. Operates daily.

Location Central Vermont, east of Brandon.

Access U.S. 7 brings traffic to Brandon. State 73 reaches east to Forestdale and signs leading to North Goshen and Blueberry Hill Farm.

Transportation Services Bus to Brandon; car rentals.

Accommodations Food and lodgings at the Farm. Also accommodations in Brandon.

Medical Assistance Rutland.

Winter Activities At the Farm skiers and their families can enjoy sledding and tobogganing on the slopes surrounding the buildings. Ice skating on a pond. Ice fishing in nearby Lake Champlain. Downhill skiing at Killington and High Pond.

(Photo by Elizabeth Presnikoff)
Learning at Stowe

Ski Touring There are about 30 miles of groomed and signed trails for NIE; mostly Intermediate. Trails lead into deep forest, over old logging roads, foot trails and special ski routes. One trail leads to Sucker Brook Shelter on the Long Trail, well located for overnight winter camping. A long tour takes skiers from the Farm to beyond Goshen and an overnight stay at Churchill Farm on State 73. A converted blacksmith shop at the Farm is now equipped to handle complete sales, rentals and waxing. Instruction here also. For all there is always "soup of the day" simmering on a pot-bellied stove. The Farm is headquarters for the Vermont Ski Touring Club.

Snowshoeing Snowshoers are welcome to use the same trails or make their own way through the woods. Advice from the Farm hosts will lead snowshoers over several enjoyable loop outings.

Winter Camping This is an important part of the program at the Farm. Ask for information about this more rugged aspect of winter outings.

Reference Blueberry Hill Farm, Brandon, Vermont 05733. Tel. (802) 247-6735.

7½' quadrangle: Brandon.

BURKE MOUNTAIN

Another complete downhill ski area that now includes facilities for ski tourers. Their program is well developed.

Season December thru mid-April. Operates daily.

Location Northeastern Vermont above St. Johnsbury.

Access I-91/U.S. 5 bring traffic to the area. State 114 leads to Burke Mountain.

Transportation Services Bus to Lyndonville.

Accommodations Food and lodgings at site and in area. Nursery.

Medical Assistance St. Johnsbury.

Ski Touring 30 miles of groomed and marked trails here for NIE. Cross-country racing. Warming hut. Overnight tours. Guided tours. Workshops. Complete sales, rentals and instruction. Nominal trail fee.

Snowshoeing Snowshers can use the same routes as ski tourers. Rentals available. Nature walks here using touring skis and snowshoes.

Downshill Skiing 4 lifts service 23 slopes and trails for NIE. 1750' VD. 1500' base el. Complete sales, rentals and instruction.

Reference Burke Mountain, East Burke, Vermont 05832. Tel. (802) 626-3305.

15' quadrangle: Burke

(Courtesy, Vermont Development Department)
Burke Mountain Tourers

VERMONT • 95

DAKIN'S VERMONT MOUNTAIN SHOP

This is a specialty shop providing service and equipment for climbers, hikers and skiers. Plenty of advice and help here.

Season   December thru March. Operates daily.

Location   Northeastern Vermont, south of Burlington at North Ferrisburg.

Access   U.S. 7 reach North Ferrisburg.

Transportation Services   Bus and airlines to Burlington; car rentals.

Accommodations   Food and lodgings nearby.

Medical Assistance   Burlington.

Ski Touring   15 miles of signed trails for NIE. 5 miles are groomed. Complete sales, rentals and instruction.

Mountaineering   Rock and ice climbing are taught here. Free indoor classes at night during the week. Field trips on weekends. All climbing equipment provided by Dakin's.

Reference   Dakin's Vermont Mountain Shop, Route 7, North Ferrisburg, Vermont 05456. Tel. (802) 877-2936.

THE FARM MOTOR INN AND COUNTRY CLUB

A family tradition is carried on here, the younger Coltures now hosts to those who enjoy country living in farm surrounds. A very unusual inn. The Mt. Mansfield and Madonna ski areas are nearby. Stowe is just south with all its amenities.

Season   Mid-December thru mid-April

Location   Northern Vermont, south of Morrisville.

Access   State 100 passes the Inn.

Transportation Services   Bus and airlines to Burlington; car rentals.

Accommodations Food and lodgings at Inn. Just south is Stowe with many lodges, inns and retaurants.

Medical Assistance Nearby.

Ski Touring 5 miles of groomed and signed trails for Novice and Intermediate. Rentals and instruction.

Reference The Farm Motor Inn and Country Club, Stowe Road (State 100), Morrisville, Vermont 05661. Tel. (802) 888-3525.

Snowshoeing Trails and open land for snowshoers. Rentals available.

Reference The Farm Motor Inn and Country Club, Stowe Road (State 100), Morrisville, Vermont 05661. Tel. (802) 888-3525.

KILLINGTON

Killington is a complete resort for Alpine skiing second to none in Vermont. Ski tourers are welcome. Wonderful spring skiing.

Season Mid-November thru April. Operates daily.

Location Central Vermont.

Transportation Services Bus and airlines to Rutland; car rentals. Bus to Killington.

Access U.S. 4 and State 4 reach Killington.

Accommodations Food and lodgings at Killington and in the area.

Medical Assistance Rutland.

Ski Touring 5 miles of trails groomed and signed for Novice and Intermediate. Warming hut. Guided tours. Complete sales, rentals and instruction.

Downhill Skiing 11 lifts service almost 4 dozen trails for NIE. 3000' VD. Complete sales, rentals and instruction.

Reference Killington, Vermont 05751. Tel. (802) 422-3333.
  7½' quadrangle: Killington Peak

MADONNA SKI AREA

Located on the crest of the Green Mountains this is a complete year-round resort. Their touring system has been improved and expanded.

Season December thru mid-April. Operates daily.

Location Northern Vermont, just south of Jeffersonville.

Access I-89 and I-91 bring traffic to the area. State 108 reaches Madonna Ski Area.

Transportation Services Bus, airlines and AMTRAK to Burlington; car rentals.

Accommodations Food and lodgings at site and nearby. Nursery.

Medical Assistance Jeffersonville.

Ski Touring 10 miles of groomed and signed trails for Novice and Intermediates. Complete sales, rentals and instruction. Guided tours.

Downhill Skiing 3 lifts service 27 slopes and trails for NIE. 1100' base el. 2600' VD. Complete sales, rentals and instruction.

Reference Madonna Ski Area, Madonna, Vermont 05464. Tel. (802) 644-8851.

7½' quadrangle: Mount Mansfield

MOUNTAIN MEADOWS LODGE

This center is another member of the North American Nordic Ski Touring System. The very best of facilities are available. The Long Trail passes near the lodge.

Season December thru March.

Location Central Vermont, east of Rutland at Killington.

(Photo by Elizabeth Presnikoff)
Mountain Meadows Lodge Ski Shop

Access U.S. 4 brings traffic to Killington and Mountain Meadows Lodge.

Transportation Services Bus to Rutland; car rentals.

Accommodations Food and lodgings at Mountain Meadows Lodge.

Medical Assistance 8 miles from Lodge.

Ski Touring 6 miles of groomed and signed trails for NIE. Complete sales, rentals and instruction.

Reference   Mountain Meadows Lodge, U.S. 4, Killington, Vermont 05751. Tel. (802) 755-2843.

MOUNTAIN TOP INN

This is a complete resort open year-round in the Green Mountains. At 2,000 feet skiers are assured good snow conditions. A very scenic area at lakeside with a mountain backdrop.

Season   Mid-December thru March. Operates daily.

Location   Eastern Vermont, north of Rutland in Chittenden.

Access   U.S. 4 and 7 lead to Rutland and north on State roads to Chittenden.

Transportation Services   Bus and airlines to Rutland; car rentals.

Accommodations   Food and lodgings at Inn.

Medical Assistance   Rutland.

Winter Activities   Ice skating, sledding and tobogganing. A Novice slope with T-bars; sales, rentals and instruction. Children's ski school.

Ski Touring   25 miles of groomed trails for NIE. Some trails signed. Mountain Top Ski Touring Club offers a nominal membership and free use of trails. Also discounts on rentals. Complete rentals and instruction.

Reference   Mountain Top Inn, Chittenden, Vermont 05737. Tel. (802) 483-2311.

7½' quadrangle: Chittenden

MOUNT SNOW

Mount Snow is a very big downhill area with all the extras. Ski tourers are welcome.

Season   December thru March. Operates daily.

Location Southern Vermont.

Access I-91 brings traffic north to Brattleboro. State 100 reaches Mount Snow.

Transportation Services None.

Accommodations Food and lodgings at Mount Snow. Another 100 inns and lodges in the area.

Medical Assistance Clinic at Mount Snow.

Winter Activities Indoor ice skating, outdoor heated pool. Horse sleighs.

Ski Touring 20 miles of trails for NIE. Old 2-mile-trail for Novice. New 18-mile trail is Intermediate and Expert on parts. Ask about ski touring at Sport Trends Ski Shop. Complete sales, rentals and instruction.

Downhill Skiing 16 lifts service almost 4 dozen trails on 3 slopes for NIE. Complete sales, rentals and instruction.

Reference Mount Snow, Vermont 05356. Tel. (802) 464-3331.
  15' quadrangle: Wilmington

OKEMO

Okemo is one of Vermont's biggest mountains. This is a very complete downhill ski resort in Ludlow ("Snow Town").

Season December thru April. Operates daily.

Location Southern Vermont.

Access I-91 brings traffic to the area. State 103 reaches Ludlow and Okemo.

Transportation Services Bus to Ludlow. Airlines to Rutland; car rentals.

Accommodations Food and lodgings at Okemo and Ludlow. This is a ski town.

Medical Assistance Springfield.

VERMONT • 101

Ski Touring   16 miles of trails groomed and signed for Novice and Intermediate. Complete sales, rentals and instruction. Guided tours.

Snowshoeing   Snowshoers are welcome. Rentals available.

Downhill Skiing   6 lifts service 22 trails for NIE. One of the wildest sections of intermediate trails in the east. 2200' VD. Complete sales, rentals and instruction.

Reference   Okemo, RFD 1, Ludlow, Vermont 05149. Tel. (802) 228-4041.
   15' quadrangle: Ludlow

SAW MILL FARM

A member of the North American Ski Touring System. Downhill skiing at nearby Mount Snow and Mount Haystack.

Season   December thru March. Operates daily.

Location   Southern Vermont in West Dover.

Access   I-91 brings traffic to the area. State 100 reaches West Dover.

Transportation Services   Bus to Brattleboro; car rentals.

Accommodations   Food and lodgings at Inn at Saw Mill Farm and in West Dover.

Medical Assistance   Brattleboro.

Ski Touring   3 miles of groomed trails for beginners. Access to many acres of skiing for NIE. Guided tours. Complete sales, rentals and instruction.

Reference   Saw Mill Ski Touring Center, The Inn at Saw Mill Farm, West Dover, Vermont 05356. Tel. (802) 464-2782.

STOWE CENTER

This ski touring center is a member of the North American Nordic Ski Touring System. If offers the tourer the best of everything.

Season December thru April. Operates daily.

Location Northern Vermont.

Access I-89 brings traffic to the area. State 100 reaches Stowe and State 108 passes Stowe Center.

Transportation Services Bus to Stowe.

Accommodations Food and lodgings in Stowe.

Medical Assistance Stowe.

Ski Touring About 15 miles of groomed and signed trails for NIE. Complete sales, rentals and instruction.

Reference Stowe Center, Box 1308, Stowe, Vermont 05672. Tel. (802) 253-4631.

15' quadrangle: Montpelier

STRATTON MOUNTAIN

A very big downhill area with everything for the skier.

Season December thru mid-April. Operates daily.

Location Southern Vermont.

Access I-91 brings traffic to the area. State 30 reaches the site.

Transportation Services Bus to Manchester; car rentals.

Accommodations Food and lodgings at site and nearby. Nursery.

Medical Assistance Stratton Mountain.

Ski Touring 12 miles of groomed and signed trails. Complete sales, rentals and instruction.

Downhill Skiing 8 lifts service 40 slopes and trails for NIE. 2125' base el. 1903' VD. Complete sales, rentals and instruction.

Reference Stratton Mountain, Vermont 05155. Tel. (802) 824-5537.

15' quadrangle: Londonderry.

Trail at Stowe Ski Touring Center

SUGARBUSH INN

A complete resort operating year-round in the Green Mountains. The Long Trail passes close to here. Downhill skiing at Sugarbush and Glen Ellen.

Season December thru March. Operates daily.

Location Northeast Vermont, west of Warren.

Access I-89 and I-91 bring traffic north. State 100 reaches Sugarbush Inn just west of Warren.

Transportation Services Bus and airlines to Montpelier and Burlington; car rentals. AMTRAK to Waterbury. Air taxi or auto taxi to Sugarbush Inn can be arranged.

Accommodations Food and lodgings at Inn and in the area.

Medical Assistance Waitsfield.

Ski Touring More than 40 miles of trails are groomed and signed here for NIE. Tour maps available at Inn. Picnic tours, moonlight tours. Complete rentals and instruction.

Reference Sugarbush Inn, Warren, Vermont 05674. Tel. (802) 496-3301.

15' quadrangle: Lincoln Mountain.

TRAPP FAMILY LODGE

This is one of the finest ski touring facilities in America. It is also one of the first of its kind to promote ski touring. Certainly it is the best known. As a complete year-round resort, the Lodge offers the very best of everything for ski tourers.

Season December thru mid-April. Operates daily.

Location Northern Vermont in Stowe.

Access I-89 and I-91 bring traffic to the area. State 100 reaches Stowe and the mountain road leading to the Lodge. Follow signs.

Transportation Services Bus to Stowe; taxi. Airlines and AMTRAK to Burlington; car rentals.

Accommodations Food and lodging at Lodge. Also food and lodgings in Stowe.

Medical Assistance Stowe.

Ski Touring Over 60 miles of groomed and signed trails for NIE. Emphasis on Intermediate and Expert routes. The main trail network was designed to provide many loops of varying lengths. In the center of the trail complex, about 3½ miles from the

Lodge, there is a warming hut with hot drinks and sandwiches. Situated as it is atop a mountain, the views from the Lodge and many of the trails are matchless. Complete sales, rentals and instruction. Guided tours. For the Expert there is a rugged 12-mile tour to the Bottom Valley Lodge, an overnight stay there, and either a tour back or a drive back. Trail maps available. Nominal trail use fee.

Snowshoeing Snowshoers are welcome, no rentals.

Reference Trapp Family Lodge, Stowe, Vermont 05672. Tel. (802) 253-7545.

15' quadrangle: Montpelier

VIKING SKI TOURING CENTER

This is another of those very special places where ski tourers will get the very best in trails, equipment and advice.

Season Mid-November thru mid-April. Operates daily.

Location Southern Vermont.

Access State 11 reached Londonderry. Little Pond Road, just east of Londonderry leads north to the ski center.

Transportation Service Bus to Manchester on U.S. 7; taxi available.

Accommodations Food and lodgings in area.

Medical Assistance Chester.

Ski Touring 20 miles of maintained and signed trails for Novice and Intermediates. Maps available. Cross-country racing. Warming hut. Guided tours, overnight tours. Complete sales, rentals and instruction. Gear rentals also includes tents, sleeping bags and packs.

Snowshoeing Snowshoers are welcome. Sales and rentals.

Reference Viking Ski Touring Center, Little Pond Road, Londonderry, Vermont 05148. Tel. (802) 824-3933.

15' quadrangle: Londonderry

WOODY'S CRACKER BARREL

One of the most popular ski shops in Vermont. The touring trails are designed to provide a variety of trips, long or short. Downhill skiing is to be had at nearby Stratton, Magic and Bromley.

Season   December thru March. Operates daily

Location   Southern Vermont in Rawsonville.

Access   State 30/100 reach Woody's Cracker Barrel Ski Shop.

Transportation Services   Bus to Manchester on U.S. 7; taxi available.

Accommodations   Food and lodgings are in the area.

Medical Assistance   Townshend.

Ski Touring   10 miles of trails groomed for Novice and Intermediates. Some signed. Complete sales, rentals and instruction.

Reference   Woody's Cracker Barrel, Londonderry, Vermont 05155.

15' quadrangle: Londonderry

VIRGINIA

There are no organized ski touring areas in Virginia—and very few downhill slopes. However, the terrain is here and while snow conditions are frequently marginal, there is good ski touring, snowshoeing, and hiking to be done.

Shenandoah National Park remains open all year with camping and access to the Appalachian Trail and the trail system within the Park. The Blue Ridge Parkway south of Shenandoah National Park is closed during the winter, providing one of the finest ski touring routes in America. As a ridgetop trail the vistas are unbelievably grand and breathtaking. It is an excellent beginners route. Any road crossing the Parkway is access.

Complete sales and rentals, with lots of help and advice is available at the Sea and Ski Shop, Ltd., 2749 McRae Road, Richmond, Virginia 23235. Tel. (703) 272-9131.

CHAPTER 3

TRAILS MIDWEST

IN THE MIDWEST good ski touring is restricted to Michigan, Minnesota and Wisconsin. Nordic activity is familiar to many of these areas because of their ethnic ties to Scandinavia. Ski jumping is very popular here, too. There was a time when our best jumpers came from these states.

While there are downhill facilities in Ohio, Indiana and Illinois, the snow there is often marginal and most areas are supported by snowmaking. Farther west Iowa, Nebraska and the Dakotas offer the easy terrain of farmlands and rolling hills. Winds and sudden severe weather can be a handicap to ski touring in the Dakotas. However, few experiences can compare with touring here on a still sunny day under a bandshell sky of blue.

For more information about ski touring in Illinois, Ohio, Michigan, Minnesota and Wisconsin write for the *Ski Touring Handbook*, $1.50, USSA Central Division, Ski Touring Com-

108 • TRAILS MIDWEST

Instruction at Boyne Mountain, Michigan

mittee, 9916 Third Avenue South, Bloomington, Minnesota 55420.

Another excellent booklet is *North Star Ski Touring Country*, $2.00, North Star Ski Touring Club, Roca Townhouses #37, 3085 Old Highway 8, Roseville, Minnesota 55113. This booklet covers ski touring areas in Michigan, Minnesota and Wisconsin.

IOWA

Usually good snow conditions prevail in the northeastern part of this state. In Postville, on U.S. 18/52 southeast of Decorah, there is a very active AYH Club, the Postville Hustlers. They do a lot of their ski touring in the Yellow River State Forest. About 30-40 miles of routes, one of which passes along a bluff overlooking the Mississippi River. Food and lodgings in Postville. For more information about touring trails contact the Northeast Iowa Council, AYH, Hall M. Roberts, P.O. Box 96, Postville, Iowa 52162.

Nearby in Castalia there is Walden Pond, a wooded hilly preserve with heated lodge and camping facilities. Ski tourers are welcome to try the very easy terrain. Write Roy Schultz, Walden Pond, Castalia, Iowa 52133.

MICHIGAN

Organized ski touring centers are few in Michigan despite its population and the affinity of residents for outdoor activities, summer and winter. The terrain is great and the snow conditions excellent. While public lands are limited in the Lower Peninsula, the Upper Peninsula provides plenty of room for touring and snowshoeing in forest lands.

For more about skiing in Michigan write for the map-folder *Michigan Winter Sports Guide,* Michigan Touring Council, Lansing, Michigan 48926.

BOYNE MOUNTAIN

This is a downhill area with complete resort facilities. Nearby there is Alpine skiing at Walloon Hills and Thunder Mountain. Boyne is the first of the big downhill areas in Michigan to develop ski touring trails.

Season December thru March. Operates daily.

Location Northern Lower Peninsula at Boyne Falls.

Access I-75 brings traffic to the area.

Transportation Services Airlines to Pellston. Bus to Boyne Falls.

Accommodations Food and lodgings at site. Heated outdoor swimming pool. Year-round ice skating. Nursery.

Ski Touring About 40 miles of trails for NIE on 4 trails. Guided tours. Complete sales, rentals and instruction.

Downhill Skiing 11 lifts service 22 slopes and trails for NIE. 600' VD. Complete sales, rentals and instruction.

Reference Boyne Mountain, Boyne Falls, Michigan 49713.

ISHPEMING

This town of 10,000 people, nestled among the low lying hills of the Marquette Range, is a popular winter sports town in the Upper Peninsula. The town's Winter Sports Club maintains a clubhouse and touring trails. The National Ski Association was founded here in 1904.

Season Mid-December thru March. Operates daily.

Location Upper Peninsula near Marquette.

Access State 28/U.S. 41 reaches Ishpeming.

Transportation Services Bus and airlines to Ishpeming.

Accommodations Food and lodgings in town.

Medical Assistance Ishpeming.

Ski Touring 12 miles of trails groomed and signed for NIE. Loop trails from clubhouse maintained by the town's Winter Sports Club. No instruction or rentals.

Reference City of Ishpeming, 100 East Division Street, Ishpeming, Michigan 49849.

A Family Thing in Boyne Country

MICHIGAN RIDING AND HIKING TRAIL

Across Michigan's Lower Peninsula, from Empire on Lake Michigan to Tawas on Lake Huron, a 210-mile trail stretches through forests and rural areas. Most of the trails are on state and federal lands. The route is primarily on or alongside dirt and abandoned roads. It is easily accessible and easily skied. There are minimal elevation changes. The trail is marked and camping is permitted. For more information contact Michigan Department of Natural Resources, Lansing, Michigan 48926. Ask for their brochure *Michigan Riding and Hiking Trails*. Or purchase the very complete booklet of county maps showing the trail; $5.00 postpaid. For information on where to get this booklet write Michigan Trail Riders, Inc., Chamber of Commerce, Traverse City, Michigan 49684.

PORCUPINE MOUNTAIN WILDERNESS STATE PARK

This is a modest downhill area in the Upper Peninsula. Beautiful mountain country along Lake Superior shore.

Season Mid-December thru March. Operates daily.

Location Upper Peninsula near White Pine.

Access State 28 brings traffic to the area.

Transportation Services None.

Accommodations Food at base lodge. Food and lodgings nearby in White Pine, Silver City and Ontonagon.

Medical Assistance White Pine.

Ski Touring 4 miles of groomed and signed trails for the Intermediate. Other unplowed roads and foot trails here are good for all classes. Complete sales and rentals.

Snowshoeing Excellent foot trails network to follow here. Vistas are magnificent from atop the mountain trails. Rentals at base lodge.

Downhill Skiing 5 lifts service 8 slopes and trails for NIE. 600′ VD. Rentals.

Reference Porcupine Mountain Wilderness State Park, Ontonagon, Michigan 49953. Tel. (906) 885-5798.
15′ quadrangle: White Pine

MINNESOTA

There are many touring possibilities around the Minneapolis-St. Paul area. Cataloging these areas is the very informative booklet published by the North Star Ski Touring Club. It lists over 30 ski touring areas. The club is very active, maintaining several miles of trails at their headquarters in Jonathan (Oakvick House). They conduct workshops and guided tours throughout the area. Write them for their booklet, $2.00, and more information about ski touring in Minnesota and Wisconsin: North Star Ski Touring Club, Roca Townhouse #37, 3085 Old Highway 8, Roseville, Minnesota 55113.

Throughout the state there are good touring possibilities in the state forest and national forests. The state parks, Pillsbury near Brainerd, Gooseberry near Two Harbors, St. Croix near Hinckley and Itasca above Park Rapids, all offer touring trails.

EQUINOX SKI TOURING CLUB

The Equinox Ski Touring Club has a touring center requiring membership for facility use. This is a "total" club with everything but overnight lodgings—a very popular place for ski touring in Minneapolis.

Season December thru March. Operates daily; night skiing.

Location Minneapolis.

Access I-35W to County 70, then west to County 8.

Transportation Services Bus and airlines to Minneapolis; car rentals.

Accommodations Food at lodge; saunas, showers and lockers. Food and lodgings in Minneapolis.

Medical Assistance Minneapolis.

Ski Touring 20-30 miles of groomed trails for NIE. Membership required. Torchlite skiing, competition, clinics. Complete sales, rentals and instruction.

Reference Equinox Ski Club, 5005 France Avenue South, Minneapolis, Minnesota 55410. Tel. (612) 929-5573.

HIDDEN VALLEY

This is winter sports area near Ely, Minnesota. Complete facilities in this town.

Season Mid-December thru March. Operates daily; night skiing.

Location Northern Minnesota at Ely.

Access I-35 and U.S. 53 bring traffic to the area.

Transportation Services None.

Accommodations Food at base lodge. Food and lodgings in Ely.

Medical Assistance Ely.

Winter Activities Toboggan chute. Ice skating, ski jumping.

Ski Touring 10 miles of groomed and signed trails for NIE. Sales and rentals.

Snowshoeing Use the base lodge as a start. Snowshoers can follow the touring trails or break out on their own.

Downhill Skiing 3 lifts service 5 hills for NIE. 180' VD. Complete sales, rentals and instruction.

Reference Hidden Valley, P.O. Box 267, Ely, Minnesota 55731. Tel. (218) 365-3097.

7½' quadrangle: Ely

SUGAR HILLS

This is a complete winter resort in Minnesota's north woods. Alpine and Nordic skiing here, along with all the amenities.

Season December thru March. Operates daily; night skiing.

Location Eastern Minnesota west of Duluth and near Grand Rapids.

Access U.S. 169 reaches Sugar Hills.

Transportation Services Bus to Grand Rapids; car rentals.

Accommodations Food and lodgings at Sugar Hills. Nursery. Pool and sauna.

Medical Assistance Grand Rapids.

Ski Touring 12 miles of groomed and signed trails for N-2, I-4, E-6. All loop trails over golf courses, along lake shores, and across mountain slopes. Maps available. Complete sales, rentals and instruction.

Snowshoeing Lots of room for snowshoeing here. Rentals available.

Downhill Skiing 9 lifts service 23 slopes and trails for NIE. 400' VD. Complete sales, rentals and instruction.

Reference Sugar Hills, Box 369, Grand Rapids, Minnesota 55744. Tel. (218) 326-3473.

7½' quadrangle: Grand Rapids.

WISCONSIN

Ideal conditions prevail in Wisconsin for good ski touring: a long winter, good snow in the northern part of the state, and wonderful open and wooded terrain for trails. The Chequamegon and Nicolet National Forests, along with the State Park System, provide excellent areas for ski touring and snowshoeing on unplowed roads, fire accesses and foot trails.

For more information about skiing in Wisconsin contact State of Wisconsin Department of Natural Resources, Box 450, Madison, Wisconsin 53701.

HARDSCRABBLE SKI AREA

A modest downhill ski area catering to family skiing. Very informal.

Season December thru March. Operates weekends and holidays; night skiing.

Location Northeastern Wisconsin at Rice Lake.

Access U.S. 53 reaches Rice Lake then 5 miles east on County C to Hardscrabble Ski Area.

Transportation Services Bus to Rice Lake.

Accommodations Food at the base lodge. Food and lodgings in Rice Lake.

Medical Assistance Rice Lake.

Ski Touring About 6 miles of groomed trails for NIE. Many more miles available in the area. No rentals or instruction.

Snowshoeing Snowshoers are welcome. No rentals.

Downhill Skiing 8 lifts service 10 slopes and trails for NIE. 350' VD. Complete sales, rentals and instruction.

Reference Hardscrabble Ski Area, Rice Lake, Wisconsin 54868. Tel. (715) 234-3412.
  15' quadrangle: Rice Lake

GATEWAY HOTEL AND INN

This hotel and inn is a complete year-round resort.

Season December thru March. Operates daily.

Location Northern Wisconsin in Land O'Lakes on Michigan border.

Access U.S. 45 reaches Land O'Lakes; car rentals.

Accommodations Food and lodgings at site.

Medical Assistance Land O'Lakes.

Winter Activities Hockey, tobogganing, sledding, sleigh riding, ice fishing, ice skating, and downhill skiing.

Ski Touring The management claims unlimited trails in Nicolet National Forest. Some are groomed. None are signed. Good for Novice skiers. Ask the management for trail suggestions. Rentals available.

Snowshoeing Snowshoers will have to be on their own as are tourers. Rentals available.

Reference Gateway Hotel and Inn, Land O'Lakes, Wisconsin 54540. Tel. (715) 547-3321.

NICOLET NATIONAL FOREST

The Vilas County Chamber of Commerce is trying to develop interest in ski touring here. At present the ski touring trail system is the one in Nicolet National Forest, just a few miles east of Eagle River.

Season December thru March. Operates daily.

Location Extreme northeastern Wisconsin.

Access U.S. 45 reaches Eagle River. State 70 passes through the Nicolet National Forest and by the parking area opposite Anvil Lake Campground.

Transportation Services Bus and airlines to Rhinelander. Car rental in Eagle River.

Accommodations Food and lodgings in Eagle River.

Medical Assistance Eagle River.

Ski Touring 5½ miles of groomed and signed trails for Intermediates. Map available. Ski shelter on the trail system. More unplowed roads to use. Sales and rentals in Eagle River.

Snowshoeing The whole forest is open to snowshoeing. Rentals in Eagle River.

Reference Vilas County Chamber of Commerce, Court House, Eagle River, Wisconsin 54521.

NOR-SKI RIDGE

A modest downhill area on the Peninsula flanking Green Bay.

Season Mid-December thru March. Operates daily; night skiing.

(Photo by Eugene A. Radloff)

Vilas County Snowshoer

Location   Extreme eastern Wisconsin northeast of Green Bay at Fish Creek.

Access   State 42/57 reaches the area.

Transportation Services   Bus and airlines to Green Bay; car rentals.

Accommodations   Food at base lodge. Food and lodgings nearby.

Medical Assistance   Sturgeon Bay.

Ski Touring   3 miles of trails with 20 miles more planned. Complete sales and rentals.

Reference   Nor-Ski Ridge, Fish Creek, Wisconsin 54212. Tel. (414) 868-3233.

15' quadrangle: Sister Bay

NORTH KETTLE MORAINE FOREST

This small forest has a completed section of the Ice Age Trail with more of it in the south section of the forest. The Ice Age Trail is a 600 mile route that will follow the edge of the most recent glacier incursion 25,000 years ago. In the forest several loop trails have been developed off the main route.

Season   December thru March. Operates daily.

Location   Eastern Wisconsin, just west of Sheboygan.

Access   U.S. 45 reaches the area. State 23, 67 and a number of other roads pass through the forest.

Transportation Services   None.

Accommodations   Food and lodgings in general area.

Medical Assistance   Sheboygan.

Ski Touring   Ski touring is designated at the Greenbrush Hiking and Skiing Trail, 4½ miles located at the Greenbrush Winter

Sports Area just south of Greenbrush on State 23. Other trails are cleared and signed.

Snowshoeing The entire trail system in the forest is available to the snowshoer.

Reference Write for maps and information, Kettle Moraine State Forest, Mauthe Lake, Wisconsin.
   15' quadrangle: Kiel, Kewaskum

PORT MOUNTAIN

A complete downhill skiing resort overlooking the Apostle Islands and Lake Superior. This is a very beautiful country for touring.

Season December thru March. Operates daily; night skiing.

Location Extreme northern Wisconsin near Bayfield.

Access State 13 reaches Bayfield and ski area.

Transportation Services Bus to Ashland; car rentals.

Accommodations Food and lodgings at Port Mountain.

Medical Assistance Washburn.

Ski Touring Over 4 miles of groomed and signed trails for NIE. Complete sales, rentals and instruction.

Snowshoeing Snowshoers take to the same trails or make their own. Rentals available.

Reference Port Mountain, Bayfield, Wisconsin 54814. Tel. (715) 799-3372.

WHITECAP MOUNTAINS

This is a very big Wisconsin downhill area, atop the Gogebic Range.

Season December thru March. Operates daily; night skiing.

Location Extreme northern Wisconsin at Montreal.

Access U.S. 51 brings traffic to Hurley and State 77 reaches Montreal.

Transportation Services Bus and airlines to Ironwood; car rentals.

Accommodations Food and lodgings at site and nearby. Ski train tours area.

Medical Assistance Ironwood, Michigan.

Ski Touring 8 miles of groomed and signed trails for NIE. Complete sales, rentals and instruction.

Snowshoeing Snowshoers are welcome here. Rentals available.

Downhill Skiing 7 lifts service 29 slopes and trails for NIE. 380' VD. Complete sales, rentals and instruction.

Reference White Cap Mountains, Montreal, Wisconsin 54536. Tel. (715) 561-2227.

7½' quadrangle: Iron Belt.

TELEMARK LODGE

A complete downhill skiing resort. Everything here for the skiers who like luxuries.

Season December thru March. Operates daily.

Location Extreme northern Wisconsin near Cable.

Access U.S. 63 reaches Cable, then 3 miles east on County M.

Transportation Services Bus to Hayward and Cable. Airlines to Hayward; car rentals.

Accommodations Food and lodgings at Telemark Lodge. Swimming pools, health center. Nursery.

Medical Assistance Hayward.

Ski Touring 12 miles of groomed and signed trails for NIE. Nominal fee. Complete sales, rentals and instruction.

Downhill Skiing 14 lifts service 11 slopes and trails for NIE. 410' VD. Complete sales, rentals and instruction.

Reference Telemark Lodge, Cable, Wisconsin 54821. Tel. (715) 798-3311.

15' quadrangle: Hayward: Namekagon Lake

CHAPTER 4

TRAILS WEST

POWDER! DEEP POWDER! Always the exultant cry of the downhill skier, often the bane of ski tourers for avalanche conditions are greater. However, for day touring through mountain forests and over plateau country, the vistas are unmatched. In the spring Alpine touring is safe and exciting.

For more information about ski touring in Colorado, Wyoming and New Mexico write for *A Guide to Ski Touring,* $3.00, Rocky Mountain Division, United State Ski Association, Ski Touring Committee, 2291 Youngfield Street, Golden, Colorado 80401.

The Colorado Mountain Club conducts workshops and tours for its members on weekends. They also run two-day trips with overnight camping. For information about the club write Colorado Mountain Club, 1723 East 16th Avenue, Denver, Colorado 80218. Tel. (303) 355-3666.

(Union Pacific Railroad Photo)
Skyline Drive Country, Utah

ARIZONA

There is not much organized ski touring done in Arizona. Downhill areas are few and touring centers are unknown at present. Williams, Arizona is just west of Flagstaff on I-40. Rolling, pine-covered hills and miles of terrain suitable for ski touring. A good deal of snowshoeing and dog sledding is done around here. A favorite run of the local people is to leave town and ski up to the Williams Ski Area, 3½ miles from town, tour the woods around the area and then return to town in late afternoon. Or make the ski area headquarters for a day of skiing the region. Food at the Williams Ski Area. Food and lodgings in Williams.

COLORADO

Colorado leads the Rocky Mountain states in downhill skiing areas and organized ski touring centers with suitable ski areas. While some of the touring trails are adjacent to downhill facilities most of them are found in public lands and national forests. There are trails suitable for all classes, along with good weather, snow conditions and matchless scenery.

Anyone ski touring in Colorado should write for the booklet, *A Guide to Ski Touring,* $3.00, Rocky Mountain Division, United States Ski Association, Ski Touring Committee, 2271 Youngfield Street, Golden Colorado 80401. The booklet describes a dozen ski touring areas; maps included.

A very excellent booklet for the Aspen area is the *Aspen Tourskiing and Cross-Country,* $2.50 Raymond N. Auger, Columbine Books, Box 2841, Aspen, Colorado 81611. Over a dozen trails with maps.

ASHCROFT SKI TOURS UNLIMITED

High above Aspen in Ashcroft, a historic ghost town, is a ski touring center that provides the very best of everything for the ski tourer. Spectacular scenery, superb skiing conditions and plenty of assistance from this outfit that exists for tourers only. Downhill skiers will find their match on nearby Aspen slopes.

Season Thanksgiving to Easter. Operates daily.

Location Western Colorado near Aspen in Ashcroft.

Access State 82 reaches Aspen. County road leads up Castle Creek to the tour center at Ashcroft.

Transportation Services Bus, train and airlines to Aspen; car rentals. Courtesy bus to Ashcroft from Aspen.

Accommodations Food and lodgings in Aspen.

Medical Assistance Aspen.

Ski Touring 20 miles of groomed and signed trails for NIE. Warming hut. Instructional tours. Day tours. Supper tours. Overnight tours and 2-day overnighters. Reservations requested. Daily trail use fee. Season tickets. Group rates. Complete sales, rentals and instruction.

Reference Ashcroft Ski Tours Unlimited, Box 1572, Aspen, Colorado 81611. Tel. (303) 925-1971.

THE ALPINEER

The Alpineer Sport Shop is headquarters in Crested Butte for ski touring. Everything here in the way of help and instruction. Tours into high country, even for beginners.

Season November thru April. Operates daily.

Location Western Colorado in Crested Butte.

Access State 135 reaches Crested Butte.

Transportation Services Bus to Crested Butte. Airlines to Gunnison; car rentals.

Accommodations Food and lodgings in Crested Butte.

Medical Assistance Crested Butte.

Ski Touring About 100 miles of trails here in the surrounding national forest for NIE. The Alpineer conducts guided tours from 1 to 4 days. Moonlight tours. Tours are learn-as-you-go, leading to old mining towns, 11,000 foot summits, warming huts, overnight stays in ghost towns and spectacular scenery. Short tours and instruction can be had at the Crested Butte Ski Area. Complete sales, rentals and instruction.

Downhill Skiing At Crested Butte Ski Area 7 lifts service 40 miles of open slopes and trails for NIE. 2100' VD. Complete sales, rentals and instruction.

Reference The Alpineer, P.O. Box 208, Crested Butte, Colorado 81224. Tel. (303) 349-5210.

PIKE NATIONAL FOREST

Southwest of Denver is the Pike National Forest and its several restricted areas that offer possibilities for ski touring and snowshoeing. Of particular interest is the Saylor Park Ski Touring Area, reached via plowed road north of Woodland Park. About 8 miles of looping trail along with plenty of chances to leave the trails and move over the gentle sloping meadows of Saylor Park. This is lodgepole pine forest. Wildlife common to the area include ravens, mule deer, snowshoe hare, squirrels and martens. Check for tracks. For more information and a map write District Ranger, Pikes Peak District, 320 West Fillmore Street, Colorado Springs, Colorado 80907.

PTARMIGAN TOURS

Close to Aspen is the Ptarmigan Tours ski touring center. This is a complete facility providing touring and racing trails for skiers. Their guided tours reach into all parts of western Colorado.

Season November thru April. Operates daily.

Location Western Colorado at Aspen.

Access State 82 reaches Aspen.

Transportation Services Bus, trains and airlines to Aspen; car rentals. Free bus to lodge and tour take-off points.

Accommodations Food and lodgings at Ptarmigan Lodge and in Aspen.

Medical Assistance Aspen.

Ski Touring 5-7 miles of groomed and signed trails for all classes on golf course adjacent to Lodge. These trails and race courses are free. Also guided tours for day and overnight in the mountains and forests around Aspen. Week-long packages. Weekly lectures and films. Snowcat and helicopter to back country tours. Complete sales, rentals and instructions.

Reference Ptarmigan Tours, Box 2976, Aspen, Colorado 81611. Tel. (303) 925-4100.

PURGATORY

This is a big downhill area with a good ski touring program. Skiing is in the very beautiful San Juan Mountains.

Season November thru April; operates daily.

Location Southwestern Colorado north of Durango.

Access U.S. 550 reaches Purgatory.

Transportation Services Bus, train and airlines to Durango; car rentals.

Accommodations Food and lodgings at Purgatory.

Medical Assistance Durango.

Ski Touring Over 30 miles of groomed and signed trails for NIE. Guided tours, one day and overnight with a stay in a ski hut. Limited party size. Complete sales, rentals and instruction. Other tours based in close-by Silverton.

Reference Durango Ski Corporation, P.O. Box 666, Durango Colorado 81301.

ROCKY MOUNTAIN EXPEDITIONS, INC.

Rocky Mountain Expeditions offers year-round activities for backpackers, ski tourers and snowshoers. Guided snowshoe and ski tours lead into the back country for day outings and as long as a week. Registration is limited. Cabin stops and Arctic tents are used on long trips. Winter mountaineering on Mt. Elbert. Custom tours available. Complete rentals for skiing gear and camping gear. Write to Rocky Mountain Expeditions, Inc., P.O. Box 576, Buena Vista, Colorado 81211. Tel. (303) 395-8466.

ROCKY MOUNTAIN NATIONAL PARK

This park straddles the Continental Divide. It is a spectacular place of snowy peaks, glaciers, Alpine plateaus and forested slopes. Excellent winter play areas. Several good ski tours for Novices and Intermediates.

Season Mid-November thru mid-April.

Location North-central Colorado above Denver.

Access U.S. 34 from Loveland to Estes Park. U.S. 36 from Boulder to Estes Park. Road open in Park from Estes Park to Hidden Valley Winter Sports Area. On the west side of the Park U.S. 40 meets U.S. 34, the route to Grand Lake and the Shadow Mountain National Recreation Area.

Transportation Services Bus to Estes Park; car rentals.

Accommodations Food and lodgings in Estes Park. Snow camping in Moraine Park. Aspenglen Campground open in winter.

Medical Assistance Estes Park.

Winter Activities Hidden Valley Winter Sports Area has very complete facilities. There is an ice rink and skate rentals. A snow-play area offers a place to use a sled, toboggan or platter. An indoor picnic area is public, as are a spectator observation lounge. A nursery is provided for day care. A cafeteria, films, illustrated lectures round out the available activities.

(Courtesy, Rocky Mt. Outfitter)

Touring South of Granby

Ski Touring Many miles of trails here for NIE. Permits required for overnight trips. Check with Rangers for trip suggestions. Guided trips are conducted by The Wilderness Outfitter, 164 South St. Vrain (Highway 7), Estes Park, Colorado 80517. Tel. (303) 586-2397. Complete sales, rentals and instruction.

Snowshoeing Snowshoers have unlimited possibilities for trips in the Park. Rentals in Estes Park.

Downhill Skiing Hidden Valley Winter Sports Area. 5 lifts service 12 slopes and trails for Novice and Intermediates. 1850' VD. Complete sales, rentals and instruction.

Reference Superintendent, Rocky Mountain National Park, Estes Park, Colorado 80517. Tel. (303) 586-4425. Special topo map: Rocky Mountain National Park, $1.50.

ROCKY MOUNTAIN SKI TOURS

Rocky Mountain Ski Tours is located in Estes Park at the Wilderness Outfitter, a complete sport shop offering guided tours, 1-2 days, snow camping, winter survival training, complete sales, rentals and instruction. Food and lodgings in Estes Park on the eastern border of Rocky Mountain National Park. For more information write Rocky Mountain Ski Tours, Box 413, Estes Park, Colorado 80517 or The Wilderness Outfitter, 164 South St. Vrain, Estes Park, Colorado 80517. Tel. (303) 586-2397.

SCANDINAVIAN LODGE

The Scandinavian Lodge, Mt. Werner Training Center, is a focal point for Nordic skiers in Colorado. The month of April brings Nordic skiers here from around the nation to attend special week long classes.

Season November thru April. Operates daily.

Location Northern Colorado near Steamboat Springs.

Access U.S. 40 reaches Steamboat Springs.

Transportation Services Bus and airlines to Steamboat Springs; car rentals.

Accommodations Food and lodgings at Lodge and in Steamboat Springs.

Medical Assistance Steamboat Springs.

Ski Touring There are about 90 miles of trails here for NIE. Some are marked and groomed. The Lodge is the start and finish of 4 prepared ski touring tracks. Weekly cross-country competition. Guided tours into the back country. Complete sales, rentals and instruction.

Snowshoeing On Mt. Werner, Steamboat or Howelson Hill.

Reference Scandinavian Lodge, P.O. Box 129, Steamboat Springs, Colorado 80477. Tel. (303) 879-0517.

SHADOW MOUNTAIN NATIONAL RECREATION AREA

This area is on the west side of Rocky Mountain National Park. It is a park of lakes—Grand Lake, Shadow Mountain Lake and Granby Lake. The backdrop is the snow-covered Continental Divide.

Season December thru April.

Location North-central Colorado adjoining Rocky Mountain National Park.

Access U.S. 40 and 34 to Grand Lake. Trail Ridge Road to Estes Park is closed.

Transportation Services None.

Accommodations Grand Lake. Snow camping at Green Ridge Campground: no water.

Medical Assistance Granby.

Ski Touring Very good for ski touring. Several trails out of Grand Lake into the Park. Touring along the east shore of the lakes. Permits are required for touring in Park. Guided tours conducted by Rocky Mountain Outfitters, Inc., Box 574, Granby, Colorado 80446. Tel. (303) 887-3777.

Reference Superintendent, National Park Service, P.O. Box 100, Grand Lake, Colorado 80447. Tel. (303) 627-3471. Special topo map: Rocky Mountain National Park, $1.50.

VAIL

Vail is a large downhill area where ski touring is very popular. The program here is well developed and the possibilities endless for touring outings. The emphasis here on ski touring rivals that of Aspen or Steamboat Springs.

Season November thru April. Operates daily.

Location Central Colorado west of Denver in Golden Peak.

Access I-70/U.S. 6 reaches Golden Peak.

Transportation Services Bus to Vail; car rentals. Airlines to Eagle; car rentals.

Accommodations Food and lodgings at Vail Ski Area.

Medical Assistance Vail Ski Area.

Ski Touring Over 20 trails and 125 miles of trails here for NIE. Guided tours for a day or longer. Some high country trails can be reached via lifts from the Vail Ski Area. Complete sales, rentals and instruction.

Downhill Skiing 16 lifts service 64 trails and slopes for NIE. 3100' VD. Complete sales, rentals and instruction.

Reference Steve Rieschl's Ski Touring School, Golden Peak, Colorado 81620. Tel. (303) 476-3116.

WILDERNESS ALLIANCE

Wilderness Alliance was founded to provide ski tourers with an organized opportunity to "promote personal growth and understanding of man's place in the biosphere." Guided tours are avail-

(Courtesy, Steve Rieschl's Ski Touring School)
Touring at Vail

able for NIE into the wilderness areas and forests of western Colorado. Trips are conducted Thanksgiving through April, including weekend outings with an overnight stop at a lodge. Longer trips of up to 5 days include stopovers at selected huts and resorts. Registration is limited on all tours. Instruction is available. For more information write the Wilderness Alliance, Route 2, Box 12D, Conifer, Colorado 80433. Tel. (303) 798-4094.

WINTER PARK

A downhill area with all the facilities to make it a grand winter resort for family skiing. This is Continental Divide country with magnificent scenery and powder snows.

Season December thru mid-April. Operates daily.

Location Central Colorado west of Denver.

Access U.S. 40 reaches Winter Park.

Transportation Services Bus to Winter Park. Bus, trail and airlines to Denver; car rentals.

Accommodations Food and lodgings in Winter Park. Nursery.

Medical Assistance Granby.

Ski Touring About 15 kilometers of groomed and signed trails for NIE. 3 routes taking 1, 3 and 4 hours to complete. NASTAR cross-country races. Also to be considered are the many miles of logging and mining roads in the surrounding Arapaho National Forest. Complete sales, rentals and instruction.

Downhill Skiing 9 lifts service 33 slopes and trails for NIE. 9000' base el. 1800' VD. Complete sales, rentals and instruction.

Reference Winter Park Ski Shop, Winter Park, Colorado 80482.

IDAHO

Ski touring is new to Idaho, but the chances are that it will become very popular in a hurry. Excellent snow conditions, the right kind of terrain in mountains and forest settings, and scenery that rivals anything in the world are sure to bring ski tourers to Idaho. The high country of the remote Salmon River Mountains, the Bitterroot Range with its Continental Divide, and National Forest areas all offer opportunities for the ski tourer.

For information about ski touring areas write for the brochure *Idaho Snow Country,* Idaho Department of Commerce and Development, Capital Building, Boise, Idaho 83707.

ROBINSON BAR RANCH

Located in the Challis National Forest on the Salmon River, this year-round resort caters to ski tourers in winter. This is the first of its kind in Idaho. More than 80 years of tending to the needs of guests surely qualifies this ranch as one of the best.

Season Thanksgiving thru mid-April. Operates daily.

Location Central Idaho, east of Stanley.

Access U.S. 93 reaches private road with horse and sleigh carrying you 2 miles to the Ranch.

Transportation Services Bus and airlines to Boise; car rentals.

Accommodations Food and lodgings at Ranch. Hot springs pool.

Medical Assistance Stanley.

Winter Activities Besides swimming in the heated pools there are sleigh rides and downhill skiing at nearby Sun Valley and Lost Trail below Salmon.

Ski Touring About 50 miles of trails for NIE. Some groomed and signed. Others routed through the Challis National Forest. Guided tours in the Sawtooth National Recreation Area. One magnificent tour takes the skier to the Ranch's out camp at Castle Peak, 11,820 feet, where two sleeping lodges provide comfortable quarters for as many days as one wants to spend in these White Cloud Mountains. Complete rentals and instruction.

Reference   Robinson Bar Ranch, Clayton, Idaho 83227. Tel. (208) 838-2354.

MONTANA

The snow is certainly here for skiers, but organized ski areas for tourers are few. The same is true of downhill skiing. Because of sparse local population the ski areas coax West Coast and Midwest skiers to the Rocky Mountains. However, for the local people there are unlimited miles of forest trails and logging roads in the National Forests. Visiting ski tourers would do well to get in touch with the U.S. Forest Service, Northern Region, Federal Building, Missoula, Montana 59801. Ask for information about possible ski touring areas in the National Forests of Montana.

BIG MOUNTAIN

Another of those very big winter resorts catering to downhill skiers. Ski touring is new here.

Season   Mid-November thru mid-April. Operates daily.

Location   Extreme northwestern Montana, north of Kalispell and beyond Whitefish.

Access   U.S. 2 and 93 reach Kalispell and Whitefish, then State 487 to ski area.

Transportation Services   Bus, airlines and AMTRAK to Whitefish; car rentals.

Accommodations   Food and lodgings at ski area. Heated outdoor pool. Nursery.

Medical Assistance   Whitefish.

Ski Touring 3 miles of groomed trails, 2 partly signed for Intermediates. Complete sales, rentals and instruction.

Downhill Skiing 5 lifts service 25 slopes and trails for NIE. 2000′ VD. Complete sales, rentals and instruction.

Reference The Big Mountain, Box 1215, Whitefish, Montana 59937. Tel. (406) 862-3511.

7½′ quadrangle: Whitefish.

BIG SKY

A big winter sports area stressing development "in partnership with nature." Ski touring, rather than downhill is stressed here.

Season December thru April. Operates daily.

Location Southern Montana above Yellowstone National Park.

Access I-90 brings traffic to the area. U.S. 191 leads south 40 miles from Bozeman to ski area.

Transportation Services Bus, airlines and AMTRAK to Bozeman; car rentals.

Accommodations Food and lodgings in the area.

Ski Touring 35 miles of groomed trails for NIE; some signed. Guided tours. Complete sales, rentals and instruction. Helicopter and Thiokol skiing.

Downhill Skiing 4 lifts service open slopes and trails for NIE. 2230′ VD. Complete sales, rentals and instruction. Helicopter and Thiokol skiing.

Reference Big Sky of Montana, Inc. P.O. Box 1, Big Sky, Montana 59716. Tel. (406) 933-4411.

BRIDGER BOWL

A complete skiing resort in the Gallatin National Forest. Touring trails are in the Forest over logging roads and access routes unplowed during winter.

(Courtesy, Big Sky of Montana, Inc.)
Getting the Hang of It

Season Mid-November thru mid-April. Operates daily.

Location Southeastern Montana, 16 miles north of Bozeman.

Access I-90 (E-W) brings traffic to Bozeman; State 293 reaches the Bridger Bowl.

Transportation Services Bus, airlines and AMTRAK to Bozeman; car rentals.

Accommodations Food and lodgings at ski area and in Bozeman.

Medical Assistance Bozeman.

Ski Touring The management says the possibilities are unlimited for NIE. Complete sales, rentals and instruction.

Downhill Skiing 4 lifts service 11 slopes and trails for NIE. Ski jump. 2200' VD. Complete sales, rentals and instruction.

Reference Bridger Bowl, P.O. Box 846, Bozeman, Montana 59715. Tel. (406) 587-1001.

15' quadrangle: Belgrade

GLACIER NATIONAL PARK

Outstanding scenery for winter activities. Perennial glaciers, more than 200 lakes amongst the peaks, and countless opportunities for ski touring and snowshoeing make this a great place for winter visitors to the area.

Season December thru March. Operates daily.

Location Northwest Montana.

Access U.S. 2 (E-W) passes along the Park's southern border to East and West Glacier.

Transportation Services Bus service to West Glacier on U.S. 2. AMTRAK to West Glacier. Airlines to Kalispell; car rentals.

Accommodations Meals and lodgings at Hungry Horse, East Glacier, St. Mary.

Medical Assistance Whitefish.

Ski Touring The Park road (10m) from West Glacier to Lake McDonald Lodge is open. Register with Rangers. Several miles of trails for NIE. On lower elevations 1 to 2 day trips can be made here. Avalanche danger.

Snowshoeing Unlimited opportunities.

Downhill Skiing At Big Mountain near Whitefish.

Reference Superintendent, Glacier National Park, West Glacier, Montana 59936. Special topo map: Glacier National Park, $1.50, contour map.

COOKE CITY

Summer skiing is very big here. The Spalding Camp at Cooke City has a complete program for racing, hot-dogging and touring. North American Nordic has come west with their expertise to provide full sales, rentals and instruction during the months of June and July. Open to those over 9 years of age. Options include biking, backpacking and pack trips. They also welcome people on a day to day basis.

Cooke City is in magnificent Yellowstone and Beartooth country, reached via one of the world's most scenic highways. The backcountry offers wild areas, excellent fishing and good fun ski touring in short-sleeve weather. For more information write the eastern base of Spalding Numero Uno Camp, 65 Cole Avenue, Williamstown, Massachusetts 01267.

LIBBY

South of Libby in the Cabinet Mountains Wilderness Area is a popular spot for ski touring and snowshoeing. No motorized traffic here. Season is from mid-November through May. Ski rentals are available in Libby, along with hospital, food and lodgings. Libby is served by AMTRAK and U.S. 2. Downhill skiing is at Turner Mountain, north of Libby; ski touring possible here also. For more information about the Cabinet Mountains Wilderness Area contact U.S. Forest Service, Flathead National Forest, Libby, Montana 59923.

NEW MEXICO

Where the Sangre de Cristo Mountains reach down from Colorado to upper New Mexico, the ski tourer will find excellent touring in the Pecos Wilderness, the Santa Fe and Carson National Forests. Further south it is ski touring atop the Sandia Mountains overlooking Albuquerque. And throughout the northern part of the state the plateau country offers skiing amongst the colorful canyons and mesas.

SANDIA RECREATION AREA

The Sandia Mountains overlook Albuquerque some six thousand feet below. The views from the crest are marvelous. A unique feature here are the conducted snowshoe hikes by Forest Rangers on the Sandia Crest. The ski area is about a half hour's drive from Albuquerque.

Season December thru March. Operates daily.

Location Central New Mexico east of Albuquerque.

Access I-25 and I-40 bring traffic to the area. State 10 and 40 reach the ski area and Sandia Crest.

Transportation Services Bus and airlines to Albuquerque; car rentals.

Accommodations Food and lodgings at ski area. Food at Sunset House at the Crest, reached via lifts from the ski area and the western foot of the Sandias.

Medical Assistance Albuquerque.

Ski Touring There are 12 miles of trails here using Forest Service trails. One such trail loops south from the Sandia Crest to the Sunset House and then returns. The Sunset House can be reached from the ski area or the base of the Sandias by tramway. An annual event is a cross-country ski race here sponsored by the New Mexico Ski Touring Club. For more information write Sandia Ranger District, Box 174, Tijeras, New Mexico 87059.

Snowshoeing Probably the first of its kind in America, the conducted snowshoe hikes along the Sandia Crest are a wonderful experience for just about anyone. During January and February forest rangers meet snowshoers at the tram base and escort them up to the Sunset House where the short interpretive hike begins. Instruction and rentals are available at the tram base. For information write the above address.

Downhill Skiing 6 lifts service 9 slopes and trails for NIE. Jumps. 1750′ VD. Base el. 8650′. Complete sales, rentals and instruction.

Reference As above.
7½′ quadrangle: Sandia Crest

SIPAPU LODGE

A year-round resort at the edge of the Pecos Wilderness. The downhill area is modest by Rocky Mountains standards, but the accommodations and scenery are all skiers could ask for.

Season Mid-December thru mid-April. Operates daily.

Location Northern New Mexico, southeast of Vadito.

Access State 3 leads to the ski area.

Transportation Services Bus and airlines to Santa Fe: car rentals.

Accommodations Food and lodgings at Lodge.

Medical Assistance Taos.

Ski Touring The trails here are many and varied, suitable for all classes. They are Forest Service roads and trails. However, most have some rather steep sections. Elevations range from 8,000 to

13,000 feet. Ask your hosts for suggested trips outlined to suit your skills. Sales and rentals.

Downhill Skiing 2 lifts service 5 trails and slopes for NIE. 437' VD. Complete sales, rentals and instruction.

Reference Sipapu Lodge, Box 29, Vadito, New Mexico 87579. Tel. (505) 587-2240.

7½' quadrangle: Tres Ritos

TAOS SKI VALLEY

This is a large downhill skiing resort with the very best of everything for those who like everything the best. Base lodge at 9,370 feet.

Season December thru April. Operates daily; night skiing.

Location Northern New Mexico near Taos.

Access U.S. 64 brings traffic to Taos. State 3 leads north to signs and the ski area.

Transportation Services Bus and airlines to Santa Fe; car rentals.

Accommodations Food and lodgings at site; also at nearby Taos.

Medical Assistance Taos.

Ski Touring There are many miles of ski touring to be had here for all classes. Some of the trails are groomed. Instruction is available.

Downhill Skiing 6 lifts service 37 slopes for NIE. 2615' VD. Complete sales, rentals and instruction.

Reference Taos Ski Valley, Box 856, Taos, New Mexico 87571.

7½' quadrangle: Arroyo Seco

TRAIL ADVENTURES DE CHAMA

This outfit specializes in backpacking and ski touring outings. They have a regular schedule of outings, offering everything for the ski tourer in this spectacular Continental Divide country around Chama.

Season November thru April; operates daily.

Location Extreme northern New Mexico north of Santa Fe in Chama.

Access U.S. 84 reaches Chama.

Transportation Services Bus and airlines to Albuquerque or Santa Fe; car rentals.

Accommodations Food and lodgings at Little Creel and Lobo Lodges, and in Chama.

Medical Assistance Chama.

Ski Touring 60 miles of groomed and partially signed trails for NIE. Clinics are featured, including meals, lodgings and equipment. Instruction, rentals and guided tours. The trail system is on a 10,000-acre private ranch with varied terrain at 7,900' to 10,000' elevations.

Reference Trail Adventures de Chama, 4839 Idlewilde Lane S.E., Albuquerque, New Mexico 87108.

UTAH

There are about a dozen large ski resorts in Utah, many of them now interested in ski touring and the development of touring trails. Some of the areas are close to national forests and their hiking/riding trails that double for touring and snowshoeing routes. Unparalleled scenery here for the ski tourer.

PARK CITY

Season Mid-November thru mid-April. Operates daily; night skiing.

(Union Pacific Railroad Photo)
Skyline Drive Country, Utah

Location   Northern Utah east of Salt Lake City at Park City.

Access   I-80 leads to the area.

Transportation Services   Bus to Park City. Airlines and train to Salt Lake City; car rentals and helicopter services.

Accommodations   Food and lodgings at ski area and Park City. Nursery. Summit house with cafeteria.

Medical Assistance   Doctor at ski area.

Ski Touring   5 miles of partially signed and groomed trails for Novice and Intermediate. Also present are old mining roads in area. Complete sales, rentals and instruction.

Downhill Skiing   9 tows service 50 slopes and trails for NIE. 2400' VD. 7000' base el. Complete sales, rentals and instruction.

Reference   Park City Resort, P.O. Box 919, Park City, Utah 84060. Tel. (801) 521-2131 and 649-9681.

SNOWLAND

This is a modest downhill area in the beautiful high country of Utah. 8,900 feet is the base elevation of this weekend resort.

Season   November thru May. Operates weekends and holidays.

Location   Central Utah east of Fairview.

Access   U.S. 89 brings traffic to Fairview, then 8 miles east on State 31.

Transportation Services   None.

Accommodations   Food at ski area. Food and lodgings in Fairview.

Medical Assistance   Mt. Pleasant.

Ski Touring   The management claims 150 miles of touring trails for NIE. Plans are to sign some of them. This is ski touring in the Skyline Drive country of Utah. Magnificent scenery.

(Courtesy, Park City Resort)

Park City Resort Tourers

Snowshoeing   The same trails are open to snowshoers here.

Downhill Skiing   Lifts service 3 slopes for Novice and Intermediates. Complete sales, rentals and instruction.

Reference   Snowland, 115 East 2nd North, Fairview, Utah 84629.

WYOMING

Wyoming ski touring can be the best. Whether it is the wonderful Big Horn Mountains or the Bridger Wilderness Area, the possibilities always offer magnificent scenery, rugged terrain and excellent weather. Spring skiing in this region will allow ski tourers some good opportunities at overnight touring in the national forests. And look for great touring in the plateau country of southern Wyoming.

For those who want to experience the ultimate in rugged winter activities there is The National Outdoor Leadership School in Lander. Courses here in winter mountaineering, glacier expeditions, ski touring and winter camping.

HAPPY JACK SKI AREA

This small downhill area is at Pole Mountain in the Medicine Bow National Forest.

Season   November thru April.

Location   Southeastern Wyoming, 10 miles east of Laramie; operates holidays and daily except Monday.

Access   I-80 brings traffic to the area.

Transportation Services   Bus, trains and airlines to Laramie; car rentals.

Accommodations   Food at the ski area. Food and lodgings in Laramie.

Medical Assistance   Laramie.

Yellowstone National Park

(Wyoming Travel Commission Photo)

Ski Touring   5 kilometers groomed and signed trails for Intermediates. Complete sales, rentals and instruction.

Downhill Skiing   2 lifts service 9 trails for NIE. 8300' base el. Complete sales, rentals and instruction.

Reference   Ski Happy Jack, Inc., P.O. Box 3722, Laramie, Wyoming 82070. Tel. (307) 745-9583.

JACKSON HOLE

A better center for ski touring cannot be found. The spectacular scenery of Jackson Hole flanked by the Tetons is one of the most impressive sights in America. The accommodations here are the very best and the town is a real fun place year-round. Ski tourers will get a chance to see great herds of wintering elk, to photograph moose, deer, coyote and the rare trumpeter swan in their winter refuge.

Season   December thru April.

Location   Western Wyoming.

Access   U.S. 89, U.S. 187/189 and U.S. 26/287 bring traffic to Jackson.

Transportation Services   Bus and airlines to Jackson; car rentals.

Accommodations   Food and lodgings at Jackson. Contact Jackson Hole Resort Association, Box 1575, Jackson Hole, Wyoming 83012. Tel. (307) 733-2774. Food and lodgings at Teton Village, Teton Village Resort Association, Teton Village, Wyoming 83025. Tel. (307) 733-4005. Winter camping is allowed at Colter Bay in Grand Teton National Park across from the Visitor's Center.

Medical Assistance   Jackson Hole.

Winter Activities   Ice fishing on Jackson, Leigh and Jenny Lakes. The Snake River has open water fishing for whitefish only.

Ski Touring Unlimited ski touring here for all classes. Permits required in Park, minimum 2 persons. Terrain is especially suited to beginners. The mass of the Tetons is seldom out of sight. Check with the Rangers at the Visitor's Center at Moose or get in touch with one of the following for a guided tour into Grand Teton, Yellowstone or the surrounding national forests.

JACK PINE SKI SHOP   Complete rentals and instruction. Half and full day tours. Lunch with all-day tours. Overnight and Alpine powder tours by arrangement. Small groups. Families welcome. Write Jack Pine Ski Shop, Box 1904, Jackson, Wyoming 83001. Tel. (307) 733-3699.

POWDERHOUND SKI TOURS   Complete rentals and instruction. Half and full-day tours. Lunch with day tours. Group rates. Write Powderhound Ski Tours, Box 752, Jackson, Wyoming 83001. Tel. (307) 733-2208.

SKI TREK XC   Complete rentals and instruction. Half and full-day tours. Overnight tours. 6-day package includes 3-4 nights at a small winter lodge on the edge of the Teton Wilderness, with instruction, day tours and overnight outing. Write Van Tribble, Ski Trek XC, P.O. Box 351, Jackson Hole, Wyoming 83001. Tel. (307) 733-4449, 733-4796.

SUNDANCE SKI TOURS   Complete rentals and instruction. Half and full-day tours. Lunch with all-day tours. Overnight and extended tours. Winter camping. Some cabins available for ski tourers. Write Sundance Ski Tours, Box 1226, Jackson, Wyoming 83001. Tel. (307) 733-4449, 733-4796.

WILDERNESS EXPEDITIONS   Complete rentals and instruction. Half and full-day tours; boots, ski poles furnished. Lunch included on full-day tours. Private, advanced powder and ski mountaineering tours. Overnight and extended tours. Several package plans. Write Wilderness Expeditions, Box 471, Jackson, Wyoming 83001. Tel. (307) 733-2258.

Snowshoeing   The snowshoer is free to move just about anywhere he wants across the valley floor and into the forests. Established foot trails provide good routes to some of the higher country.

Downhill Skiing There are 2 downhill areas: Snow King in Jackson Hole and the ski area at Teton Village with its aerial tram ride to 10,450 feet atop Rendezvous Peak. Both these areas offer the best in slopes and accommodations. They can also be a base of operations for those who ski tour as well as take to the slopes. For information write, Snow King, P.O. Box R, Jackson, Wyoming 83001. Tel. (307) 733-2851, or contact Teton Village Resort Association, Teton Village, Wyoming 83025. Tel. (307) 733-4005.

Reference Jackson Hole Travel Service, P.O. Box 96, Jackson, Wyoming 83001. Ask for information of interest to a ski tourer or snowshoer. Also write for the map-brochure of the Grand Teton National Park, Moose, Wyoming 83012. A topo map is available from the same address, $1.50 postpaid.

MEDICINE BOW SKI AREA

Situated in the Snowy Range of southern Wyoming this small downhill facility is the favorite of many of this part of Wyoming. Easy driving from Cheyenne and Laramie.

Season November thru April. Operates Thursday thru Sunday and long holidays.

Location Southeastern Wyoming 4 miles west of Centennial.

Access I-80 brings traffic to the area. State 130 leads to ski area.

Transportation Services Bus, trains and airlines to Laramie; car rentals.

Accommodations Food at ski area base lodge. Food and lodgings in Centennial.

Medical Assistance Laramie.

Ski Touring 10 kilometers of groomed and signed trail for Intermediates and Experts. University of Wyoming Ski Team trains

(Medicine Bow Ski Area Photo)

University of Wyoming Nordic Racers

here; they sponsor NCAA races and maintain the track. Complete sales, rentals and instruction.

Downhill Skiing   4 lifts service 11 runs and a ski jump for NIE. 700' VD. 8500' base el. Complete sales, rentals and instruction.

Reference   Medicine Bow Recreation, Inc., Centennial, Wyoming 82055. Tel. (307) 745-9511.

7½' quadrangle: Centennial

SHOSHONE NATIONAL FOREST

Northwest of Dubois about 20 miles of U.S. 26/287, in the Wind River District, there is an area closed to motorized vehicles in order to provide snowshoeing and ski touring in a secluded spot. Use the parking lot at Tie Hack Monument.

YELLOWSTONE NATIONAL PARK

Our first national park, Yellowstone is a wonder in winter dress. This high plateau country, with the backdrop of the Continental Divide, is an excellent area for ski touring and snowshoeing. Visitors can reach the many hot springs and geysers, survey the broad plains and enjoy the presence of elk, bison, moose, big horn sheep, deer and the occasional grizzly from a distance.

Season   December thru April.

Location   Northwest Wyoming.

Access   From the north via U.S. 98 to Gardiner, then on to Mammoth. The Park road is open from Mammoth east to Cooke City. Via U.S. 191 to West Yellowstone. Via U.S. 89 from Jackson through Grand Teton National Park to the South Gate.

Transportation Services   Airlines to Bozeman, Montana. Bus and AMTRAK to Livingston, Montana. Concessioner bus service meets airlines, bus and rail services on advance reservation. Write Yellowstone Park Company, Yellowstone National Park, Wyoming 82190. Tel. (307) 344-7321.

Accommodations Food and lodgings at Gardiner, West Yellowstone and Jackson. Food and lodgings at the Snow Lodge near Old Faithful and the Visitor's Center, reached via snowcoach from the above towns. Package trips available. This is one of the very best ways to see Yellowstone. Winter camping at Madison Campground near West Yellowstone.

Medical Assistance Jackson.

Ski Touring Endless opportunities for ski touring on your own or with the help of guides (see listings under Jackson Hole). Instruction and rentals are available at the Snow Lodge.

Snowshoeing The same freedom of movement for skiers is here for snowshoers. Open plateaus, quiet forest trails and good snow conditions make this ideal snowshoeing country.

Reference Superintendent, Yellowstone National Park, Wyoming 82190. Special topo map: Yellowstone National Park, $1.50. Also contact Yellowstone Park Company at the above address. Tel. (307) 344-7311.

A wonderful booklet is published by the Yellowstone Library and Museum Association, Yellowstone National Park, Wyoming 82190: *Winter Comes to Yellowstone* by Stanley G. Canter, 25 cents postpaid.

CHAPTER 5

TRAILS FAR WEST

GENERALLY NORDIC SKI touring has been slow to develop in the Far West. However, Alpine ski touring and mountaineering have been practiced for many years, much of this restricted to late winter and spring skiing. The heavy snowpacks on the Cascades and Sierras allows early summer skiing on several summits.

Ski touring on an organized basis, either at downhill areas or ski touring centers is not as well developed here as in the East. For the most part touring and snowshoeing are done at lower levels than the Rocky Mountains, yet higher than the East. However, the people out here feel that theirs is the very best ski touring. While those from other regions will debate them, they will be hard pressed to prove that the scenic splendor coupled with the long season and usual good weather of the Far West can be beat.

OREGON

The Cascades with their blanketing national forests offer many opportunities for the ski tourer. Ski touring centers are developing fast and the open hill country flanking the Cascades allows for plenty of day outings. The high country scenery is splendid. To be touring in sight of peaks like Mt. Hood, The Three Sisters or Mt. Jefferson is a memorable trail experience.

For a guide to ski touring in central Oregon check out *A General Guide to Central Oregon Cross-Country Skiing,* by the Bend Chapter of the Oregon Nordic Club. About 30 pages, with trail ratings. $1.00 at ski shops in Bend, Oregon.

ANTHONY LAKES

This modest downhill ski area has a well developed ski touring program.

Season Mid-November thru April. Operates Wednesday through Sunday and holidays.

Location Eastern Oregon, west of North Powder.

Access I-80N and U.S. 30 bring traffic to North Powder. Follow signs to ski area.

Transportation Services Bus to ski area from Baker.

Accommodations Food at ski area. Food and lodgings at North Powder and Baker.

Medical Assistance Baker.

Ski Touring About 36 miles of trails here for Novice and Intermediate. Spring tours; 5-days into Elkhorn Range; old mining towns. Overnight cabins. Complete sales, rentals and instruction.

Downhill Skiing 2 lifts service 11 slopes and trails for NIE. 900' VD. Complete sales, rentals and instruction.

Reference Anthony Lakes Corporation, P.O. Box 1045, Baker, Oregon 97814. Tel. (503) 523-2492.

COOPER SPUR

On the north side of Mt. Hood, Cooper Spur is in the "weather lee" of the mountains where the days are sunnier and the snow is powder. A small but very popular family downhill ski area. Skiing on Mt. Hood originated here.

Season Mid-December thru March. Operates Thursday through Sunday and holidays.

Location Northern Oregon, southwest of the town of Mt. Hood.

Access State 35 reaches Mt. Hood and paved road leading to ski area.

Transportation Services None.

Accommodations Food at ski area. Food and lodgings at Hood River.

Medical Assistance Hood River.

Ski Touring 4 trails from 6 to 20 miles are groomed and signed for NIE. Wide open, protected slopes above and below timberline for touring. Rentals available.

Snowshoeing Snowshoers are welcome to use the trails at Cooper Spur.

Downshill Skiing 2 lifts service trails and slopes for NIE. Rentals and instruction.

Reference Cooper Spur, Inc., Hood River, Oregon 97031. Tel. (503) 386-2777.

CRATER LAKE NATIONAL PARK

Few places in the world can compare with this beautiful winter site: snow-covered trees, crater walls and sky reflected in the deep blue lake. This, the second deepest lake in the western hemisphere, is a wonderful ski touring area.

Season December thru May.

Location Southern Oregon in the Cascade Range.

Access U.S. 97 and State 62 lead to the Park. Crater rim drive closed in winter.

Transportation Services None.

Rentals None.

Accommodations Food on weekends in Park at Rim Village.

Medical Assistance Park first aid.

Ski Touring Trails around lake. Unplowed roads in Park; tour the lake perimeter. Overnight trips possible, permits required.

Snowshoeing As above.

Reference Write for information about winter activities, Superintendent, Crater Lake National Park, P.O. Box 7, Crater Lake, Oregon 97604. Special topo map: Crater Lake National Park, $1.00.

DIAMOND LAKE

Diamond Lake, in the Umpqua National Forest, is just north of Crater Lake National Park. Bordering on the lake is a large area closed to motorized travel. It provides good Alpine ski touring and snowshoeing. The Tipsoo and Thielsen Trails lead up to the Pacific Crest Trail. Food and lodgings at Diamond Lake Resort on State 138. Both trails have access and parking at snowmobile unloading lots. For map of the area write for *Diamond Lake Snow Trails*, District Ranger, Diamond Lake District, Toketee Route, Box 101, Idleyld Park, Oregon 97447. Tel. (503) 498-2531.

HOODO BOWL

A downhill area on the crest of the Cascades at Santiam Pass.

Season Mid-November thru mid-May. Operates daily.

Location Central Oregon, northwest of Bend.

Access U.S. 20 leads to the ski area.

Transportation Services Bus to ski area.

(Lee Fischer and Al Warren)

Touring around Bend, Oregon

Accommodations Food at ski area.

Medical Assistance Bend.

Ski Touring 30 miles of groomed and signed trails for NIE. Nordic and Alpine ski touring. The Pacific Crest Trail and the trails around Three Fingered Jack are accessible from here. Overnight trips can be planned.

Snowshoeing As above.

Downhill Skiing 7 lifts service 10 slopes and trails for NIE. 1035' VD. Complete sales, rentals and instruction.

Reference Hoodo Ski Bowl, Box 20, Highway 20, Sisters, Oregon 97759.

MT. BACHELOR SKI AREA

This is a big downhill ski area very much interested in the ski tourer. Their program is well developed and offers lots of help and suggestions for ski tourers.

Season December thru April.

Location Central Oregon south of Bend.

Access U.S. 97 reaches Bend, then State 46 west to ski area.

Transportation Services Bus and airlines to Bend; car rentals.

Accommodations Food and lodgings at ski lodge.

Medical Assistance Bend.

Ski Touring At the ski area there are 2 looping trails of one and two miles for Novice skiers and the NASTAR races held regularly. In the area just north of the ski area several trips have been outlined by the ski school: 4 to 20 miles return for all classes. Guided tours. Complete sales, rentals and instruction.

To the west the Three Sisters Wilderness is an area well suited to ski touring. In the same area the annual John Craig Memorial Cross-Country Ski Tour and Ski Race is held in April, an 18-mile route across McKenzie Pass on State 242. The race commemorates the pioneer spirit of John Templeton Craig who died in a 1877 blizzard while delivering the mail on skis over McKenzie Pass. A tour precedes the race.

Downhill Skiing   5 lifts service open slopes and trails for NIE. Platter pull. 1600' VD. Complete sales, rentals and instruction.

Reference   Mt. Bachelor Ski Area, Route 3, Box 450, Bend, Oregon 97701.

SPOUT SPRINGS

A downhill ski area with all the amenities for northeastern Oregon skiers.

Season   November thru March. Operates daily, except Monday, Night skiing.

Location   Northeastern Oregon, northeast of Pendleton.

Access   I-80N brings traffic to the area. State 11, 82 and 204 lead to the ski area just east of Weston.

Transportation Services   Bus and airlines to Pendleton; car rentals.

Accommodations   Food and lodgings at site.

Medical Assistance   Pendleton.

Ski Touring   10 miles of signed trails available. No instruction or rentals. This was the 1964 training site for our Olympic Nordic Cross-Country Race team.

Snowshoeing   Use the same trails. Rentals available.

Downhill Skiing   5 lifts service 9 slopes and trails for Novice and Intermediates. 550' VD. Sales, rentals and instruction.

Reference   Spout Springs, Inc., Route 1, Weston, Oregon 97886. Tel. (503) 566-2015.

SUNRIVER

Sunriver is a residential development offering a very complete program of winter and summer activities. The lodge here is the center of things. Food and lodgings available. 74 miles of trails for NIE. Good tours for beginners; round trip outings. One trail leads 17½ miles from Sunriver to Mt. Bachelor Ski Area. Nearby Three Sisters Wilderness also provides routes for tours. Complete rentals and instruction along with showshoe rentals. Season is December thru March. Sunriver is located on the Deschutes River just south of Bend, Oregon. U.S. 97 reaches road leading to Sunriver. For more information contact Sunriver Properties, Inc., Sunriver, Oregon 97701. Tel. (503) 593-1221.

TRILLIUM LAKE BASIN

Just south of Mt. Hood is the Trillium Lake Basin with its snow trails for skiers and snowmobiles. Park at Snow Bunny Lodge on U.S. 26. Several miles of trails on unplowed summer roads. Generally rolling hill country with no steep hills. Routes are from 4½ to 14-mile loops. Good views of Mt. Hood to the north. For more information and a map-brochure write Forest Supervisor, Mt. Hood National Forest, P.O. Box 16040, Portland, Oregon 97216.

WASHINGTON

A maritime climate brings Washington a good deal of heavy, wet snow along the western Cascade slopes and over the Olympics. The singular volcano peaks of the northwest with their accompanying forest are impressive backgrounds for all manner of winter activities.

Containing dozens of ski tours and ski areas the publication *Northwest Ski Trails,* by Mueller, $4.95 is a must for ski tours in this area. The tours described are mainly Alpine touring and mountaineering, but a few are easy enough to be classed as Nordic tours.

For snowshoers there is Prater's, *Snowshoe Hikes,* $3.95, outlining over 80 snowshoe trips in the Cascades and Olympics, from a day's outing to rigorous week-long tours including mountaineering.

For both of the above books write The Mountaineers, P.O. Box 122, Seattle, Washington 98111.

49°NORTH

Excellent snow conditions here, more sunny days than at ski areas farther west. This new downhill area is located in the Kaniksu National Forest east of the Columbia River.

Season Mid-November thru mid-April. Operates daily.

Location Northeastern Washington above Spokane at Chewelah.

Access U.S. 395 reaches Chewelah. Follow signs to ski area.

Transportation Services Bus and airlines to Spokane; car rentals.

Accommodations Food and lodgings at site and Chewelah. Nursery.

Medical Assistance Chewelah.

Ski Touring About 10 miles of trails for Novice and Intermediate. Some are signed. Guided tours. Complete sales, rentals and instruction.

Downhill Skiing 3 lifts service 15 miles of slopes and trails for NIE. 2000' VD. Complete sales, rentals and instruction.

Reference 49° North, 327 Old National Bank Building, Spokane, Washington 99201. Tel. (509) 624-5247.

MISSION RIDGE

A big downhill area with trails developed for ski touring. Wenatchee Valley College conducts courses here. The snow is drier and days sunnier here on the eastern side of the Cascades.

(Courtesy, Mission Ridge)

Clinic for NASTAR Racers

Season December thru May. Operates daily.

Location Central Washington, 12 miles south of Wenatchee.

Access U.S. 2, U.S. 97 and State 28 reach Wenatchee. Follow signs to ski area.

Transportation Services Bus and airlines to Wenatchee; car rentals.

Accommodations Food at ski area. Food and lodgings in Wenatchee.

Medical Assistance Wenatchee.

Ski Touring 9 miles of groomed and signed trails (3) for NIE. Guided tours. NASTAR cross-country races. Complete sales, rentals and instruction.

Snowshoeing A 15-mile trail from Mission Ridge is described in *Snowshoe Hikes*.

Downhill Skiing 7 lifts service 25 slopes and trails for NIE. 2 ski jumps. 2140' VD. Complete sales, rentals and instruction.

Reference Mission Ridge, P.O. Box 542, Wenatchee, Washington 98801.

MT. BAKER

A large downhill ski area open all year. Ski school operates during summer.

Season Mid-November thru May. Operates weekends and holidays. Summer skiing.

Location Extreme northwestern Washington.

Access I-5 and State 542 bring traffic to Mt. Baker.

Transportation Services None.

Accommodations Food at ski area. Food and lodgings in nearby Glacier and Maple Falls.

Finishing Telemark Turns

(Courtesy, Mission Ridge)

Ski Touring Several miles of trails here leading out from the ski area. Suitable routes for all classes, Nordic and Alpine touring. Check with ski area for possible routes, some of them away from the area on forest roads near Glacier.

Downhill Skiing 9 lifts service 45 trails and slopes for NIE. 1500' VD. Complete sales, rentals and instruction.

Reference Mt. Baker Ski Area, 2014 Moore Street, Bellingham, Washington 98225. Also see *Northwest Ski Trails*.

MOUNT RAINIER NATIONAL PARK

Rising to a height of 14,410 feet Mount Rainier dominates the Park. The ice-clad peak is a magnificent view above the forested slopes. The Paradise Ski Area is an inexpensive family spot, with good touring possibilities.

Season December thru April.

Location Western Washington near Tacoma and Seattle.

Access I-5 and I-90 bring traffic to the area. Only State 7 and 706 bring traffic to winter sports area. State 123 passes through the western portion of the Park but there are no winter facilities. Stevens Canyon Road, Paradise to State 123, is closed.

Transportation Services None to Park. Bus and airlines to Seattle and Tacoma; car rentals.

Accommodations Food and lodgings near Park entrance at Nisqually. Snow camping at Sunshine Point near Nisqually entrance. Warming shelter at Paradise Visitor Center open on weekends and holidays: snackbar.

Medical Assistance Park first aid.

Winter Activities Snow-play area at Paradise Ski Area; tubes and platter sliding.

Ski Touring Several trails for the Alpine ski tourer; easy to most difficult. Nordic touring can be done on a limited basis on the slopes above the ski area. Check with Rangers.

Snowshoeing Snowshoers will generally stick to the same established routes as the ski tourer.

Downhill Skiing Paradise Ski Area, open weekends and holidays. 5 lifts service trails and slopes for NIE. Rentals and instruction.

Reference Superintendent, Mount Rainier National Park, Longmire, Washington 98397. Tel. (206) 569-2211. Special topo map: Mt. Rainier National Park, 80 cents postpaid. Also see *Northwest Ski Trails* and *Snowshoe Hikes*.

OLYMPIC NATIONAL PARK

The ski area at Hurricane Ridge on the northern edge of the Park offers good touring. The vistas are magnificent, including the mountains and the sea on either hand. The Cascades and the summits on Vancouver Islands may be seen in good weather.

Season Mid-December thru mid-April. Facilities open only during weekends and holidays.

Location Northwest Washington.

Access U.S. 101 circles the Park.

Transportation Services Bus and airlines to Port Angeles; car rentals.

Accommodations Food at ski area. Food and lodgings in Port Angeles. Snow camping permitted.

Medical Assistance Port Angeles.

Winter Activities A snow play area for sleds, toboggans, tubes and platters is located at Hurricane Ridge Ski Area.

Ski Touring About 21 miles of trails here for all classes. Alpine and Nordic touring here on open, sub-Alpine ridge tops: 1 to 2 day trips. Overnight hut available by reservation. Sales and rentals.

Snowshoeing Snowshoers follow the same routes as ski tourers. Sales and rentals.

Downhill Skiing 3 lifts service slopes for NIE. Sales and rentals and instruction.

Reference Superintendent, Olympic National Park, Port Angeles, Washington 98362. Special topo map: Olympic National Park, $1.00. Also see *Northwest Ski Trails* and *Snowshoe Hikes*.

WENATCHEE NATIONAL FOREST

The Forest Service has developed trails here for touring and snow-shoeing—and snowmobiling! However, there are trails restricted to ski touring and snowshoeing, especially around the Lake Wenatchee Winter Recreation Area, located in central Washington along U.S. 2. Some ridge touring available here; 15' quadrangle: *Wenatchee Lake*. Food and lodgings in the area. For maps and information about ski touring or snowshoeing in this area contact Wenatchee National Forest, P.O. Box 811, Wenatchee, Washington 98801.

CALIFORNIA

Much of California ski touring, both Nordic and Alpine ski touring has been done on a do-it-yourself basis. There are few organized ski touring centers as in eastern states. However, things are changing. An excellent winter climate—plenty of snow on the mountains and terrain like Kirkwood Meadows, Mammoth Lakes and Yosemite Valley bring out the Nordic ski tourers.

Ski touring has developed in the Lake Tahoe area. Resorts like Northstar, Squaw Valley and Heavenly Valley provide sales and rentals along with instruction and guided tours. The Sierra Club has a winter sports facility at Norden in the Donner Pass skiing area. Members are provided food and lodgings with access to Nordic and Alpine trails in the area. Several downhill ski resorts nearby. Use of these facilities requires membership in the Sierra Club, 1050 Mills Tower, San Francisco, California 94104.

For those who want to get out on their own, either to begin with or after lessons from a ski touring center, there is the very excellent book, *Ski Tours in California,* David Beck, $4.95, Wilderness Press, 2440 Bancroft Way, Berkeley, California 94704. This describes over three dozen trails and touring areas in California.

ALPINE MEADOWS

A large family ski resort in a magnificent Sierra setting. A program designated The Wilderness Experience is conducted here for Alpine and Nordic skiers, racing enthusiasts, winter campers and mountaineers.

Season Mid-November thru April. Operates daily.

Location Eastern California just west of Tahoe City.

Access I-80 brings traffic to the area. State 89 reaches access to ski area; follow signs.

Transportation Services Bus to Tahoe City. Airlines to Reno; car rentals.

Accommodations Food at ski area. Food and lodgings in Truckee or Tahoe City. Nursery.

Medical Assistance Truckee.

Ski Touring Over 40 miles of groomed and signed trails are available here and in the vicinity of NIE. Guided tours 1-4 days. Complete sales, rentals and instruction.

Downhill Skiing 12 lifts service open slopes and trails for NIE. 1600' VD. Complete sales, rentals and instruction.

Reference Alpine Meadows, P.O. Box AM, Tahoe City, California 95730. Tel. (916) 583-4232.

BOREAL RIDGE

Downhill skiing in the northern Sierras at the very popular Donner Pass skiing area.

Season Mid-November thru mid-April. Operates daily. Night skiing.

Location Eastern California, west of Lake Tahoe.

Access I-80 reaches the ski area.

Transportation Services Bus to Tahoe City. Airlines to Reno; car rentals.

Accommodations Food at ski area. Food and lodgings nearby.

Medical Assistance Truckee.

Winter Activities Snow play area for sleds, platters and toboggans.

Ski Touring Many miles of trails in the vicinity of NIE. Guided day tours. Complete sales, rentals and instruction.

Snowshoeing Snowshoers are welcome to the area. Rentals available.

Downhill Skiing 10 lifts service 15 slopes and trails for NIE. 600' VD. Jump. Complete sales, rentals and instruction.

Reference Boreal Ridge, P.O. Box 39, Truckee, California 95734. Tel. (916) 426-3666. See also: *Ski Tours in California.*

CAL-NORDIC SKI TOURING INSTITUTE

The Tamarack Lodge is headquarters for this ski touring center. A very complete operation working in partnership with Kirkwood Ski Touring Center at Kirkwood. The Mammoth Lake area is excellent ski touring country.

Season Mid-November thru May. Operates daily.

Location East-central California, west of Mammoth Lakes.

Access U.S. 395 brings traffic to the Mammoth Area. The Tamarack Lodge is just northwest of Mammoth Lakes.

Transportation Services None.

Accommodations Food and lodgings at Tamarack Lodge and in Mammoth Lakes.

Medical Assistance Mammoth Lakes.

Ski Touring 25 miles of signed trails for NIE. Some are groomed. Ski touring clinics. Guided tours, 1-2 days, featuring a swim in hot springs. Moonlight tours. Retailers clinics. Instructors certification program. Racing program. Ski mountaineering. Snow camping and survival classes. Complete sales, rentals and instruction.

Reference Cal-Nordic Ski Touring Institute, Tamarack Lodge, Mammoth Lakes, California 93546. Tel. (714) 934-6955.

DONNER SKI RANCH

Another complete downhill ski area in the Lake Tahoe district.

Season Mid-December thru April. Operates daily; night skiing.

Location Eastern California, west of Lake Tahoe.

Access I-80 reaches area and State 40 leads to site.

Transportation Services Bus to nearby Soda Springs. Train to Truckee; car rentals.

Accommodations Food and lodgings at site.

Medical Assistance Truckee.

Ski Touring 4 miles of trails for Intermediate. Complete sales, rentals and instruction.

Snowshoeing Trails and rentals available.

Downhill Skiing 4 lifts and tows service a variety of trails for NIE. Complete sales, rentals and instruction.

Reference Donner Ski Ranch, P.O. Box 66, Norden, California 95724. Tel. (916) 426-3578.

KIRKWOOD SKI TOURING CENTER

A very complete ski touring center at a major ski resort in the Sierras. A base elevation of 7,800 feet insures drier snow and a longer season than many skiing resorts in California. This is wonderful ski touring atop Kirkwood Meadows.

Season November thru April. Operates daily.

Location Eastern California below Lake Tahoe.

Access State 88 reaches Kirkwood, about 35 miles south of South Lake Tahoe.

Transportation Services Bus and airlines to South Lake Tahoe; car rentals. Shuttle bus from South Lake Tahoe to Kirkwood.

Accommodations Food and lodgings at Kirkwood and South Lake Tahoe.

Medical Assistance South Lake Tahoe.

Ski Touring 25 miles of signed trails for NIE. 10 miles are groomed. Guided tours, 1-2 days. Moonlight tours. Ski touring clinics. Race program. Retailers clinic. Instructors certification program. Ski mountaineering. Snow camping and survival classes. Complete sales, rentals and instruction.

Downhill Skiing 4 lifts service slopes and trails for NIE. 200' VD. Complete sales rentals and instruction.

Reference Kirkwood Ski Touring Center, Kirkwood,

California 95646. Tel. (209) 258-8541. See also: *Ski Tours in California*.

LASSEN VOLCANIC NATIONAL PARK

Lassen Peak has been an active volcano in this century. Rising as a singular peak, snow-covered and grand, Lassen is a focal point for extensive winter activities. The ski touring program here is well developed.

Season Mid-December thru March. Open daily.

Location North-central California in the Southern Cascades.

Access I-5 brings traffic to the area. State 44 and 36 lead to Park road.

Transportation Services Bus to Mineral, daily except Sunday. Airlines to Redding; car rentals.

Accommodations Food at Lassen Chalet in Park. Food and lodgings in Mineral and Childs Meadow. Snow camping in Park.

Medical Assistance Park first aid.

Winter Activities Tobogganing is done here on an informal basis. Pick your slope. Use tubes and platters.

Ski Touring Several marked trails for NIE. Group instruction. Guided tours; 1-4 days. Winter camping and mountaineering. Rentals available. Operating on weekends and holidays.

Snowshoeing Snowshoers are welcome at the Park.

Downhill Skiing 3 lifts service open slopes and trails for NIE. 600′ VD. Rentals and instruction. Operating on weekends and holidays.

Reference Superintendent, Lassen Volcanic National Park, Mineral, California 96063. Special topo map: Lassen Volcanic National Park, 75 cents.

SEQUOIA AND KINGS CANYON NATIONAL PARKS

Winter brings a beauty to these parts that rivals the grandeur of summer scenery. Snow-clad mountains, giant sequoias, and great stretches of wilderness make this a favorite wintering spot for many.

Season December thru March. Open daily.

Location East-central California in the Sierra Nevadas.

Access State 99 brings traffic to the area. State 180 and 198 reach Grant Grove and Giant Forest.

Transportation Services Bus, trains and airlines to Fresno; car rentals. Bus service available from Fresno to Park with advance reservation. Write Concessioner, Sequoia and Kings Canyon National Parks, Sequoia National Park, California 93262. Tel. (209) 565-3421.

Accommodations Food in Park. Food and lodgings at Giant Forest, Wilsonia at Grant Grove, Stony Creek Lodge north of Giant Forest. Camping at Potwisha. Snow camping in parking areas at Lodgepole and Grant Grove. Pear Lake Ski Hut can be reached via a 6-mile ski trail from Wolverton; advance reservation needed. Tel. (209) 565-3341.

Winter Activities Sleds, tubes and platters are allowed at Wolverton, Lodgepole and Grant Grove. Ice skating at Lodgepole on weekends.

Ski Touring There is ski touring at both access points to the Parks. At times of heavy snowfall the Generals Highway between the entrances will be closed. Several tours are available on marked trails from either end. Check with Rangers and Wolverton winter use area.

Snowshoeing The Parks are open to snowshoeing.

Downhill Skiing 3 rope tows, rentals and instruction at Wolverton winter use area.

Reference Superintendent, Sequoia and Kings Canyon National Parks, Three Sisters, California 93271. Tel. (209) 565-3301. Special topo map: Sequoia and Kings Canyon National Parks, $1.00. Also see: *Ski Tours in California*.

YOSEMITE NATIONAL PARK

Yosemite Valley is an outstanding scenic attraction in winter. Unlike many parks and recreation areas, most of Yosemite can be visited in winter. The valley floor has year-round accommodations and the Badger Pass Ski Area is the hub of ski touring activity.

Season Mid-December thru mid-April. Operates daily.

Location East-central California in the Sierra Nevada Mountains.

Access State 120 from Modesto, State 140 from Merced, State 41 from Fresno.

Transportation Services Bus service to Yosemite Valley and Badger Pass Ski Area. Bus and airlines to Fresno and Merced; car rentals. Shuttle bus in Park.

Accommodations Food and lodgings in Yosemite Valley. Nursery at Badger Pass Ski Area. Snow camping permitted with registration at a ranger station. Campgrounds open in Yosemite Valley.

Medical Assistance Yosemite Valley.

Winter Activities Aside from all the very pleasant amenities in restaurants, lounges and game rooms, a variety of outdoor winter playing is found here. At Curry Village there is ice skating. A snowplay area, sleds and platters at Badger Pass. Guided tours throughout the Park. Sleigh rides in Yosemite Valley when the moon is full.

Ski Touring 60 miles of signed trails, plus 60 miles of unplowed roads for NIE. The valley floor or the high country is accessible. Nordic and Alpine ski touring. Guided tours 1-3

(Courtesy, Yosemite Park & Curry Co.)
Ostrander Lake Ski Hut

days using ski huts; registration limited. Nordic racing instruction. Complete sales, rentals and instruction.

Snowshoeing As above for trails. Rentals. Snow camping and guided trips.

Downhill Skiing At Badger Pass Ski Area there are 4 lifts servicing 21 slopes and trails for NIE. 980' VD. Complete sales, rentals and instruction.

Reference Superintendent, P.O. Box 577, Yosemite National Park, California 95389. Tel. (209) 372-4456. Special topo map: Yosemite National Park, $1.00. Also see: *Ski Touring in California*.

INDEX

Acadia National Park,
  Maine 50
Adirondak Loj, New York 75
Akers Ski, Maine 52
Alpineer, The, Colorado 126
Alpine Meadows,
  California 172
Anthony Lakes, Oregon 158
Appalachian Mountain Club,
  Massachusetts 48
ARIZONA 125
Ashcroft Ski Tours Unlimited,
  Colorado 125

Balsams Wilderness Ski Area,
  New Hampshire 65
Bark Eater, New York 79
Bear Mountain State Park,
  New York 78

Big Mountain, Montana 137
Big Sky, Montana 138
Big Tupper Ski Area,
  New York 79
Blueberry Hill Farm,
  Vermont 91
Blue Knob Ski Area,
  Pennsylvania 90
Blue Ridge Parkway,
  Virginia 106
Boreal Ridge, California 173
Boyne Mountain,
  Michigan 109
Bridger Bowl, Montana 138
Burke Mountain, Vermont 93

CALIFORNIA 171
Cal-Nordic Ski Touring
  Institute, California 173

182 • INDEX

COLORADO 125
CONNECTICUT 48
Cooke City, Montana 141
Cooper Spur, Oregon 159
Crater Lake National Park,
  Oregon 159
Cross Country Ski Place,
  Maine 53
Crystal Lake Camp and
  Conference Center,
  Pennsylvania 87

Dakin's Vermont
  Mountain Shop,
  Vermont 95
Dartmouth Outing Club,
  New Hampshire 66
Diamond Lake, Oregon 160
Donner Ski Ranch,
  California 174

Elk Mountain Ski Center,
  Pennsylvania 88
Equinox Ski Touring Club,
  Minnesota 113
Erie Bridge Cross Country
  Ski Center, New York 80

Farm Motor Inn and Country
  Club, Vermont 95
Fo'castle Farms, New York 81
49° North, Washington 165
Franconia Inn,
  New Hampshire 66
Franconia Notch State Park,
  New Hampshire 67
Frost Ridge, New York 82

Gateway Hotel and Inn,
  Wisconsin 116
Glacier National Park,
  Montana 140
Granville State Forest,
  Massachusetts 58
Gray Ledges,
  New Hampshire 68

Happy Jack Ski Area,
  Wyoming 149
Happy Valley Ski Center,
  New York 82
Hardscrabble Ski Area,
  Wisconsin 115
Hartwell Hill Ski Area,
  Massachusetts 58
Hidden Valley, Minnesota 114
Hoodo Bowl, Oregon 160

IDAHO 136
Inlet and Old Forge,
  New York 83
IOWA 109
Ishpeming, Michigan 110

Jackson, New Hampshire 68
Jackson Hole, Wyoming 151
Jug End Resort,
  Massachusetts 59

Killington, Vermont 96
Kirkwood Ski Touring Center,
  California 175

INDEX

Lassen Volcanic National Park,
   California   176
Libby, Montana   141
Loon Mountain,
   New Hampshire   70

Madonna Ski Area,
   Vermont   97
MAINE   50
MARYLAND   56
MASSACHUSETTS   57
Medicine Bow Ski Area,
   Wyoming   153
MICHIGAN   109
Michigan Riding and
   Hiking Trail   111
MINNESOTA   112
Mission Ridge,
   Washington   165
Mr. Moose Outfitters,
   New York   83
MONTANA   137
Mountain Meadows Lodge,
   Vermont   97
Mountain Top Inn,
   Vermont   99
Mount Airy Lodge,
   Pennsylvania   88
Mt. Bachelor, Oregon   162
Mt. Baker, Washington   167
Mount Rainier National Park,
   Washington   169
Mount Snow, Vermont   99

New Germany State Park,
   Maryland   56
NEW HAMPSHIRE   63
NEW JERSEY   62
NEW MEXICO   142
NEW YORK   75

Nicolet National Forest,
   Wisconsin   117
Nor-ski Ridge, Wisconsin   117
North Kettle Moraine Forest,
   Wisconsin   119

Okemo, Vermont   100
Olympic National Park,
   Washington   170
OREGON   158

Park City, Utah   145
PENNSYLVANIA   86
Peoples State Forest,
   Connecticut   48
Pike National Forest,
   Colorado   127
Pine Ridge Ski Area,
   New York   84
Pinkham Notch Camp,
   New Hampshire   70
Pittsfield State Forest,
   Massachusetts   60
Porcupine Mountain Wilderness
   State Park, Michigan   112
Port Mountain, Wisconsin   120
Powderhound Ski Tours,
   Wyoming   152
Powder Ridge Ski Area,
   Connecticut   49
Ptarmigan Tours,
   Colorado   127
Purgatory, Colorado   128

Robinson Bar Ranch,
   Idaho   136
Rocky Mountain Expeditions,
   Colorado   129

INDEX

Rocky Mountain National
  Park, Colorado   129
Rocky Mountain Ski Tours,
  Colorado   131
Rum Runner Ski Touring
  Center, New York   84

Sandia Recreation Area,
  New Mexico   142
Saw Mill Farm, Vermont   101
Saylor Park Ski Touring Area,
  Colorado   127
Scandinavian Lodge,
  Colorado   131
Sequoia and Kings Canyon
  National Parks,
  California   177
Seven Springs,
  Pennsylvania   89
Shadow Mountain National
  Recreation Area,
  Colorado   132
Shenandoah National Park,
  Virginia   106
Shoshone National Forest,
  Wyoming   155
Sipapu Lodge,
  New Mexico   143
Snowland, Utah   147
Spout Springs, Oregon   163
Squaw Mountain, Maine   54
Stokes State Forest,
  New Jersey   63
Stowe Center, Vermont   101
Stratton Mountain,
  Vermont   102
Sugarbush Inn, Vermont   103
Sugar Hills, Minnesota   114
Sugarloaf/USA, Maine   54
Sunriver, Oregon   164
Swain Ski Center,
  New York   85

Taos Ski Valley,
  New Mexico   144
Telemark Lodge,
  Wisconsin   121
Temple Mountain Ski Area,
  New Hampshire   72
Trail Adventures de Chama,
  New Mexico   145
Trapp Family Lodge,
  Vermont   104
Trillium Lake Basin,
  Oregon   164

UTAH   145

Vail, Colorado   133
VERMONT   91
Viking Ski Touring Center,
  Vermont   105
VIRGINIA   106

WASHINGTON   164
Waterville Valley,
  New Hampshire   73
Waubeeka Spring,
  Massachusetts   61
Wenatchee National Forest,
  Washington   171
West Mountain, New York   86
Whitecap Mountains,
  Wisconsin   120
Wilderness Alliance,
  Colorado   133
Wilderness Expeditions,
  Wyoming   152
Williams Ski Area,
  Arizona   125
Windblown,
  New Hampshire   74

Winter Park, Colorado 135
WISCONSIN 115
Woody's Cracker Barrel,
  Vermont 106
Wyckoff Park Ski Touring
  Center, Massachusetts 62

WYOMING 149

Yellowstone National Park,
  Wyoming 155
Yosemite National Park,
  California 178